The Economics of International Development

THE ECONOMICS OF INTERNATIONAL DEVELOPMENT

Foreign Aid versus Freedom for the World's Poor

WILLIAM EASTERLY

with commentaries by

ABIGAIL R. HALL-BLANCO

CHRISTIAN BJØRNSKOV

SYLVIE ABOA-BRADWELL

Institute of
Economic Affairs

First published in Great Britain in 2016 by
The Institute of Economic Affairs
2 Lord North Street
Westminster
London SW1P 3LB
in association with London Publishing Partnership Ltd
www.londonpublishingpartnership.co.uk

The mission of the Institute of Economic Affairs is to improve understanding
of the fundamental institutions of a free society by analysing and expounding
the role of markets in solving economic and social problems.

A CIP catalogue record for this book is available from the British Library.

ISBN 978-0-255-36731-8

Many IEA publications are translated into languages other
than English or are reprinted. Permission to translate or to reprint
should be sought from the Director General at the address above.

Typeset in Kepler by T&T Productions Ltd
www.tandtproductions.com

Printed and bound in Great Britain by Hobbs the Printers Ltd

CONTENTS

4   William Easterly's challenge to the development community   55

A commentary on William Easterly's lecture

Christian Bjørnskov

5   Entrepreneurship, social engagement and African development in the twenty-first century   73

A commentary on William Easterly's lecture

Sylvie Aboa-Bradwell

Sylvie Aboa-Bradwell

Sylvie Aboa-Bradwell is an award-winning entrepreneur, writer and educator. She is the founder and CEO of Medzan Training, a leadership and self-development training company. She has designed courses that provide leadership, self-development and motivational sessions to entrepreneurs, professionals and young people. She is also the founder and director of the Policy Centre for African Peoples.

Before founding the Policy Centre for African Peoples and Medzan Training, Sylvie Aboa-Bradwell served as UK Director of the Centre for Democracy and Development, a Nigeria-based think tank, for over three years. Before that, she worked for institutions promoting human development, education and rights in Africa, Britain, Spain and elsewhere for nearly 10 years.

Christian Bjørnskov

Christian Bjørnskov is Professor of Economics at Aarhus University in Denmark. He is also affiliated with the Research Institute of Industrial Economics in Stockholm, the Centre of Political Studies in Copenhagen, Denmark, and the Institute of Economic Affairs. Bjørnskov obtained his PhD from the Aarhus School of Business. His main research interests include long-run development processes, the economic consequences of informal institutions, as well as happiness economics. His research has been published in journals such as the *Journal of Economic Behavior and Organization*, *Public Choice*, the *Journal of Development Economics* and *Academy of Management Perspectives*. He is a regular columnist at the Danish financial newspaper *Børsen* and a member of the editorial boards of *Public Choice* and the *European Journal of Political Economy* (http://pure .au.dk/portal/da/chbj@asb.dk).

William Easterly

William Easterly is Professor of Economics at New York University and Co-Director of the New York University Development Research Institute, which works to bring high-quality economic research to the problems of world poverty. He has previously worked for the World Bank, the Institute for International Economics and the Centre for Global Development. Professor Easterly has been listed by various magazines as one of the world's most highly cited researchers, as one of the top 100 global intellectuals and as one of the top 100 scientist stars of Twitter.

He has written a number of books about foreign aid and its effect on developing countries. His most recent book, *The Tyranny of Experts*, was a finalist for the Manhattan Institute's Hayek Award (which he previously won in 2008 for his book *The White Man's Burden*).

Abigail Hall-Blanco

Abigail Hall-Blanco is Assistant Professor in Economics at the University of Tampa in Florida and a Research Fellow with the Independent Institute, a non-partisan research and educational think tank based in Oakland, California. She is an affiliated scholar with the Foundation for Economic Education. Blanco earned her PhD in economics from George Mason University in Fairfax, Virginia, in 2015. Her broader research interests include Austrian economics, political economy and public choice, defence and peace economics, and institutions and economic development. Her work includes topics surrounding the US military and national defence, including domestic police militarisation, arm sales, weapons as foreign aid, the cost of military mobilisation and the political economy of military technology. She is currently researching how foreign intervention adversely impacts domestic political, social and other institutions as well as pursuing additional research on policing in the US.

FOREWORD

In late 2015, the IEA was delighted to welcome Professor William Easterly to give the IEA Hayek Memorial Lecture. Easterly is a renowned academic and commentator who is especially interested in the plight of the world's poorest peoples. Earlier in his life, he believed that the plight of the poor could be improved by development assistance from abroad. However, he became disillusioned as a result of his experiences and also as his understanding of economic theory developed.

Easterly's work is extremely relevant to current debates in the UK and worldwide. Since 2010, the UK government has implemented a pledge to increase government spending on foreign aid to 0.7 per cent of national income. This is not an uncontroversial pledge. There are those, of course, who believe that it is wrong to use taxpayers' money for such a purpose even if aid could do some good for the world's poorest countries. However, there are many others who believe that the record of foreign aid is at best patchy and that it may do a great deal of harm. Still others complain that a monetary target for aid spending will lead to waste and inefficiency in a rush to spend the money so that the target is met.

Much of the evidence suggests that, on balance, aid can do some good – but the good that it does is probably small. However, as Christian Bjørnskov shows in his commentary on Easterly's lecture, aid is certainly neither a necessary or sufficient condition for development. Many countries have developed with very little or no foreign aid (especially in Asia). Other countries, such as Zambia, have received huge amounts of foreign aid (never dropping below 10 per cent of national income for 20 years from the mid-1980s) and yet have stagnated. Other large aid recipients have become poorer. The best that can be said is that aid has provided a sticking plaster and might have some small benefits. Bjørnskov suggests that some types of projects might, on balance, be helpful, though in the aggregate it is difficult to be optimistic about the success of aid.

There are downsides to foreign aid. For example, aid might actually encourage the kind of poor governance that can lead to disastrous economic, social and political outcomes. Aid can encourage rent seeking. It can also undermine the relationship between a government and its peoples because the government does not need to turn to an electorate to raise taxes to fund spending. Even more alarmingly, one study has suggested that foreign aid between 1960 and 1999 might have almost doubled the level of arms spending in Africa.

Overall, therefore, it might be the case that aid could bring about small benefits for a recipient country. But, on the other hand, if the risks of providing foreign aid materialise, the costs could be enormous. The problem is that we do not know in advance whether aid will be successful or not. The kind of centralised planning that comes with aid and leading development from out-side a country may bring about all sorts of unforeseen consequences.

And this is the root of the problem according to Easterly. Foreign aid involves planners trying to find technical solu-tions to a country's underdevelopment. The development movement certainly has no shortage of 'plans' – and the same plans have been wheeled out time and time again for decades. And they fail. What is needed instead, Easterly believes, is the promotion of human rights to allow people to be responsible for their own development.

Easterly is optimistic given the increase in the number of democracies in Africa in the last few years and the re-duction in wars. As Easterly puts it: 'Technical solutions do not happen by themselves. They happen in an en-vironment of rights, including economic rights, in which people can choose how to use their own land for them-selves or for their business customers'. In other words, we do not have the knowledge to plan for development from outside. Instead, we need the conditions in place in which people can make their own plans harnessing the know-ledge which is naturally dispersed among the people and which cannot be centralised. The commentary by Sylvie Aboa-Bradwell takes forward this idea. She discusses the contribution of organisations that can assist poor people – specifically in Africa – to be responsible for their own development.

It might reasonably be asked why aid is perpetuated if it does not work. The second commentator, Abigail Hall-Blanco, provides one answer: rent seeking. Many of those involved in the aid process (development institutions such as the World Bank; charities such as Oxfam; and aid recipient governments) have a strong incentive to lobby for more aid, regardless of whether it works.

William Easterly is also strongly opposed to military intervention. Such intervention has, he argues, rarely done any good (including in colonial times) and has done a great deal of harm. Often such intervention ends up supporting the very people who trample upon the rights of their citizens thus preventing the conditions for successful development from arising.

Abigail Hall-Blanco, also takes forward this theme. Indeed, in many ways, the problems with military intervention are the same as those with foreign aid – we do not know in advance what works. We simply do not have the knowledge to plan military interventions with any certainty that they will be successful: the situation on the ground is too complex. Recent examples illustrate this well. Furthermore, those in charge of the military are often in a position to pursue 'rent-seeking' behaviour. That is, they will use the channels of government to promote their own interests. Perhaps it should be noted that such people are not necessarily acting in a selfish way: they might, as a result of their position, simply overestimate the chances of success and underestimate the importance of dispersed on-the-ground knowledge in resolving civil conflict.

In Western societies, there is a widespread view that governments should provide some assistance to those who do not have the essentials necessary for a dignified life, such as food, shelter, clothing, healthcare and basic primary education for children. Certainly, you can argue that the development of the world's poorest peoples should be an important issue for economists – after all, we should surely be more interested in how people below the breadline can increase their income by 10 per cent per year for 20 years than whether economic growth in the UK next year is 1.5 per cent or 1.6 per cent. Furthermore, given the awful conditions that many people experience under dictators, we should take an interest in whether or not military action can improve their lot. But, as the authors of this short book make clear, the issues are complex. Development cannot necessarily be 'done' from the outside. Both aid and military intervention might do more harm than good. People who make such points are not uncompassionate. Preventing politicians from doing harm and pointing out that there is no 'magic bullet' solution to problems of poverty is, itself, an important service for economists. As such, William Easterly in his Hayek lecture and the three commentators make an important contribution to our understanding of poverty. The IEA is pleased to recommend this text to students, teachers and all who take an interest in the plight of the world's poorest people.

The views expressed in this monograph are, as in all IEA publications, those of the authors and not those of the Institute (which has no corporate view), its managing trustees, Academic Advisory Council members or senior staff. With some exceptions, such as with the publication of lectures, all IEA monographs are blind peer-reviewed by at least two academics or researchers who are experts in the field: this publication is one such exception.

PHILIP BOOTH

Academic and Research Director,
Institute of Economic Affairs,
Professor of Finance, Public Policy and Ethics,
St. Mary's University, Twickenham

August 2016

ACKNOWLEDGEMENTS

The IEA would like to thank CQS for its very generous sponsorship of the 2015 Hayek Memorial Lecture and of this publication.

SUMMARY

- Hopes for development aid remain high among Western politicians and pundits, but the evidence is depressing. Foreign aid has on average probably no effect on long-run growth.
- To understand the failure of many development projects, we need a deeper consideration of the failure of top-down planning in general, a lesson Hayek taught. Without the mechanisms of free markets and entrepreneurial actions to guide them, development agencies and governments are consistently unable to determine which projects will be successful and which will fail.
- Foreign aid and development efforts often focus exclusively on technical solutions to the problem of poverty. There is a 'technocratic illusion' that we can ignore politics, and the battle of values between freedom and dictatorship. But, as economists or as development workers, we cannot do our work in a value-free, politics-free environment.
- Even during the times of slavery, the British and Americans made specious technocratic arguments that slavery somehow made slaves better off, for example in relation to diet. Concern for the rights of the poor should be universal and should be a

non-partisan and bipartisan effort in free societies that value the rights for themselves.

- We should not be hypocritically criticising dictators in Africa without looking at our own role in the US and the UK in supporting dictators to promote our own foreign policy interests while ignoring the rights of poor Africans that are being violated. The problem of poverty is not a shortage of experts: it is a shortage of rights.

- When there is an environment of universal rights for poor people, then technical solutions can happen. In the absence of those rights, there will be no incentive to bring about technical solutions on a permanent basis.

- Despite these problems, freedom is making gradual progress in Africa. The ratio of democrats to dictators among African leaders is rising. Consequently, since the mid 1990s, Africa has had very healthy economic growth.

- There is still too much poverty, but the trends are in the right direction and the fastest progress against poverty is being made precisely because of the advance in political and economic freedom around the world.

- We need to convince fellow voters in the US and the UK that our own aid agencies should not violate the rights of the poor, our own foreign policy should not violate the rights of the poor, and our own military should not violate the rights of the poor. We should look at ourselves to see if we are complicit in violating the rights of the poor.

- One neglected area of development policy is advocacy for more freedom for poor people, for more political and economic rights: this should be our focus.

TABLES AND FIGURES

1   THE TYRANNY OF EXPERTS: FOREIGN AID VERSUS FREEDOM FOR THE WORLD'S POOR

William Easterly

Technocrats and the failure of development policy

I do not need to convince you that there is still going on in our world today a battle of values between freedom and dictatorship. The sad thing for me, as a development economist, is that a lot of us who work in aid and development – and I count my own past self in this – have too often unintentionally ended up on the side of the dictators. This happened by accident. It was certainly contrary to the private sympathies of most of us who work in aid and development who believed in freedom over dictatorship, but it happened because foreign aid and development efforts often focus on technical solutions alone to the problem of poverty.

There is something about technical solutions that is very seductive. It sounds very plausible that a lot of the problems of the poor could be fixed with some appealingly simple technical intervention. Let us suppose that a group of farmers are raising food inefficiently on their land and a forestry project could come in and deliver a lot higher value for the same land. Or suppose people are suffering from malnutrition and part of their problem is vitamin A deficiency which can be alleviated very cheaply and simply by vitamin A capsules. Or suppose the same people are suffering from malaria, which can be treated with a variety of technical weapons in our arsenal, including just spraying a chemical called pyrethrum that kills mosquitoes on the walls of houses. Or even clean water: it is as simple as drilling a well to the water table.

These technical solutions seem so straightforward and simple that there is an illusion that we can just specify the technical solutions and then they will happen and poverty will be solved. That is what we could call the 'technocratic illusion': that we can ignore politics, and ignore the battle of values between freedom and dictatorship.

Let me tell you a story about how that technocratic vision can go badly wrong. This is a story that happened on 28 February 2010 in a district called Mubende, Uganda, where a group of farmers were in church when they heard gunfire outside. They went outside and they found men with guns burning down their houses and torching their crops. Their guns were going off because the men were shooting the villagers' livestock. They marched these 20,000 farmers away from their own land at gunpoint and told them: 'The land is no longer yours'. This land had been in their families for generations. Why was this happening?

These events were actually happening because of a World Bank forestry project that had promoted what was believed to be a better use of the land – forestry rather than the use for which the farmers had been using it. You can see that a simple technical solution such as forestry is not so simple after all and that we do need to talk about things like the rights of poor people. Of course, when it came to the farmers in Mubende, Uganda, every possible right was grossly violated. Their property rights, their political rights to protest against the violation of their property rights and their human rights were infringed.

The saddest thing to me about this story is that, even though this story became much more publicised than almost any other rights violation in the history of development (it actually showed up on the front page of the *New York Times*), nothing happened. The World Bank was momentarily embarrassed that they had sponsored a project that dispossessed 20,000 farmers at gunpoint and promised the next day to do an investigation. It has been almost six years since that event happened and the World Bank never did that investigation: they never investigated their own role in that tragedy. What is even sadder to me is that nobody in the development and aid world really protested much about this at the time.[1] There was almost silence: and so the World Bank really got away scot-free with a massive rights violation of poor Ugandans.

---

1   The Compliance Advisory Ombudsman (CAO) did write a report on these events following a complaint by Oxfam. The CAO reports to the President of the World Bank. The report was not an investigation of the World Bank because it did not cover the Bank's own role and actions and the report also emphasised that it 'does not make any judgment on the merits of the complaint and the issues therein.' CAO staff have reported to this author that they do not have the mandate to investigate the World Bank itself. The CAO's role and cases can be found at http://www.cao-ombudsman.org/.

At this point, as an economist, I almost feel as if I have to apologise for talking about an emotional issue such as farmers being dispossessed at gunpoint and human rights violations. Economists usually do prefer to talk in technical terms and not to talk about values and issues.

As Hayek said in a famous quote in a discussion at the American Enterprise Institute in the late 1970s: 'the neglect by economists to discuss seriously what is really the crucial problem of our time is due to a certain timidity about soiling their hands by going from purely scientific questions into value questions'. Talking about an emotional, compelling issue such as human rights, political rights and economic rights, I feel as if I am almost confessing that I cry at the end of Hollywood romance comedies (which I actually do). I want to convince you that this is a cause that economists should take seriously and that indeed everyone in the aid and development world should take seriously.

Why is this? It is because, as economists or as development workers, we actually cannot do our work in some kind of value-free, politics-free environment. At the most elementary level, there is a concept in economics called 'revealed preference'. If someone chooses A over B, we can assume that they must be better off because they had the choice and they took A over B. That is an extremely roundabout way of saying that economists think they were the ones to discover that people are only better off doing something if they consented to that something. But, I think that was previously obvious before economists came along.

The reverse is true, also. If coercion was necessary to impose something on some Ugandan farmers, then obviously they were worse off, because coercion would not have been necessary if they had thought they would be better off.

That is the elementary underlying logic of why we cannot ignore such a simple principle as the rights of the poor to choose: to choose their own destiny, to possess their own property, and to be able to protest if you violate that choice and that right to consent. That is why we cannot ignore politics in development work.

We should also rid ourselves of the notion that this argument could be perceived as self-righteous. It is not. I, myself, for most of my career subscribed to the technocratic illusion that I am criticising tonight. I was embarrassingly late in coming around to the realisation that it does not make sense.

When we have this debate about rights, we are also often told that we are being partisan or ideological. But, this is not the property of one political party or another. The concern for the rights of the poor should be universal and should be a non-partisan and bipartisan effort in free societies that value the rights for themselves. We value our own rights for ourselves. We should value rights for poor people.

This incident in Uganda is not an isolated incident. It actually is something that goes back deep into the history of Africa, from which there are many stories which involve some combination of a Western power involved in Africa aligned with some local oppressors who violate the rights of poor Africans.

On this occasion, one reason that the World Bank got away with it is that the dictator of Uganda, Yoweri Museveni, is a big ally of the US and the UK in the war on terror. That is one reason why the giving of loans to Uganda – even violating rights and even supporting directly a rights violation in its own projects – is something that the World Bank can get away with. It is because of that political environment – that is another political reality that we cannot ignore.

We should not be hypocritically criticising dictators in Africa without looking at our own role in the US and the UK in supporting dictators to promote our own foreign policy interests without valuing the rights of poor Africans that are being violated. This history, of course, also goes back deep into colonial times, when Western colonial powers were aligned with local intermediaries and the Western colonial powers were, themselves, the oppressors and the autocrats violating the rights of the poor.

It so happens that, in colonial times, there was also a technocratic approach to solving the problems of the poor. I will illustrate that with a table (see Table 1). I obtained the information from a very long technocratic report on Africa that was actually published in 1938 by a British colonial official. The official, Lord Hailey, prepared this 1,000-page technocratic report on how to solve poverty in Africa, and the solutions that he came up with sound remarkably similar today.

You remember that chemical called pyrethrum that you spray on the walls of houses to kill the mosquitoes? That was already known in 1938. The idea of vitamin A supplements to deal with malnutrition was already known

Table 1 **Technocratic solutions to poverty 1938 and 2005**

African problem to be addressed	Solution: African Survey 1938	Solution: UN report 2005
Malaria	Spraying native huts with pyrethrum	Indoor spraying (pyrethroids)
Malnutrition	Address deficiency of vitamin A	Address inadequate intake of vitamin A
Clean water	Sinking boreholes	Increase boreholes

in 1938. Table 1 compares the recommendations from the 1938 report with the same recommendations that were made in a United Nations report in 2005 that was prepared or publicised by some famous economists you've probably heard of. I am trying to remember some of the names: Jeff Sachs, Angelina Jolie, Bono, the world's leading aid economist...

Anyway, they were the authors or publicists of the UN report, the counterpart to Lord Hailey. They came up with the same solutions in 2005 that he had already come up with in 1938.

The moral of this table is that, if you thought that problems of poverty could be solved by expert solutions and by experts, there were already experts in 1938 that already knew the answers. It did not work then and it's not working now.

The importance of 'rights'

The problem of poverty is not a shortage of experts: it is a shortage of rights. There is a very long literature in economics in which rights are, themselves, a problem-solving mechanism that makes the technical solutions happen. It is the ability of us as free citizens in our own societies and it is the ability of poor people in their societies to hold the suppliers of their needs, both private and public, accountable that makes technical solutions happen.

Technical solutions do not happen by themselves. They happen in an environment of rights, including economic rights, in which people can choose how to use their own land for themselves or for their business customers. You can hold private suppliers accountable by driving them out of business if they don't supply your needs. We can hold the government suppliers of goods such as clean water accountable through political protest and through democratic elections.

In such a 'rights environment', rights do indeed bring about development. They do not do so perfectly. There is never any utopia on the horizon. But when there is an environment of universal rights for poor people and for citizens of a society, then, indeed, that does make technical solutions happen. In the absence of those rights, there will be no incentive to bring about the technical solutions on a permanent basis.

Of course, technical solutions do form a convenient justification for a lot of US and UK foreign policy. In justifying support for autocrats in the war on terror, it can be awfully convenient also to be saying: 'Well, we're making development happen by supporting those autocrats in those poor countries. We're making development in Uganda happen by giving aid to Museveni.'

We seem to get a 'two-for-one' in that we get both our ally in the war on terror and we also get development happening by giving development aid to the dictator. Well, I am sorry to disabuse you of this being a new idea, but Lord Hailey already had that idea in 1938. He offered colonial rule as a way to get development and for the British also to get to keep their empire, which, at the time, they wanted to keep. He made a statement that the British Empire was 'part of the movement for the betterment of the backward peoples of the world'. That language has probably not been used that way today exactly ('the betterment of the backward peoples of the world'), but we have recast the same idea.

Lord Hailey made the argument, without any particular evidence, that poor people do not care about their political rights. He said: 'Political liberties are meaningless unless they can be built up on a better foundation of social and economic progress'. That was a convenient justification for continuing the empire and continuing colonialism. It was actually already being disproved at the time by all the poor people in Africa who were fighting for the end of colonial rule.

There was a drama that was played out then that is often replayed now when British humanitarians at the time in 1938 asked: 'What should we do to end poverty?' This is always the big question in the field of global poverty. Lord Hailey wanted to say, 'Look at the technical solutions over here. But please ignore the political realities of colonialism over there'. And he wanted to perpetrate the technocratic illusion that the solutions can be followed through without worrying about those messy political issues like colonialism. He wanted the experts like me to give an answer along the lines of: 'Spray native huts with pyrethrum, give vitamin A capsules and sink boreholes.' He did not want me to say, 'Just end colonialism', though this actually ended up happening against the will of the colonial powers.

Today, we are in a somewhat analogous situation. Let me give you one other example of an ally in the war on terror, another dictator, Meles Zenawi of Ethiopia. In his long rule, until he died from natural causes in 2012, he was a big ally of the US and of the UK in the war in terror, and it was a very convenient justification that he could also be seen as a development leader and that he was helping develop Ethiopia.

The major aid donors to Ethiopia were DFID from the UK, USAID and the World Bank. Not only that, but the Gates Foundation – I'll get to Mr Gates in a moment – is also a huge supporter of Ethiopia. Now, I don't really have time to give you too many atrocity stories in today's talk. But, sadly, there is one from Ethiopia, which also involved forced resettlement financed by USAID, DFID and the World Bank, in which there was a programme that forced farmers in the province of Gambela at gunpoint away from their lands. It is basically an exact replay of the Mubende story in Uganda.

Despite all that, once again, the technocratic illusion is to ignore these rights violations and concentrate on the tangible solutions such as those in Table 1. Mr Gates is a good example of that. He praised the Ethiopian government in 2013 for 'setting clear goals, choosing an approach, measuring results, and then using those measurements to continually refine our approach'. Gates said that this 'helps us to deliver tools and services to everybody who will benefit'. He has also said that he had 'a great working relationship with

[Ethiopian autocrat] Meles Zenawi, who has made real progress in helping the people of Ethiopia'. Gates is very much embracing the technocratic illusion here.

He seems unaware of the argument that dictators actually do not cause progress. They cause poverty. Dictators are the reason that poverty is there in the first place. Following a long history of previous autocracy, of colonial rule, and of the slave trade we should be supporting the end of the reign of autocracy, not its continuation supported with development aid.

So, having criticised technocratic action plans to end poverty, the next question is, what is my own technocratic action plan to end poverty? I don't have one. I am one expert who refuses to give an action plan. Why would I refuse? One reason is that we already have quite a large surplus of action plans. A lot of them are sitting on shelves, unread. This has actually been documented by the World Bank's own researchers. The World Bank thinks of itself as the knowledge bank that comes up with all these action plans. A recent study by a couple of World Bank authors found that 31 per cent of the World Bank's 'knowledge products' have never been downloaded; and 87 per cent were never cited. 'Never cited' means, basically, nobody ever read them.

Making progress on economic freedom and political rights

The history of progress on rights suggests another force that may be a candidate to consider as an alternative to action plans: 'advocacy'. How do we make progress on rights?

There is actually a long history of advocacy of moral norms, caring about the things that we are not supposed to care about in the technocratic world view. Advocates made progress by asserting that slavery was wrong; that colonialism was wrong; that government violations of human rights, such as those that happened in Mubende, Uganda, were wrong; that segregation was wrong; and that racism was wrong.

Martin Luther King Jr's most famous speech was called 'I Have a Dream'. It did not go down in history as 'I Have an Action Plan'.

So far, this has been a somewhat gloomy story. But, in the final part of the talk, I want to give you some good news. Despite the sad history of aid and of development people not caring about the rights of the poor, there is another group of people that do care about the rights of poor people: that is poor people.

Poor people fighting for their own rights have much more patience and resolve than we, as outside sympathisers, do. And they have made a lot of progress already, in Africa as well as elsewhere. There is a new book called *Africa Uprising*, which documents more than 90 political protests in 40 African countries in the past decade. As a result of this, freedom is making gradual progress in Africa. In 1988, there were far more dictators than there were democratically elected governments in Africa. In 2012, there are still more dictators than democratically elected governments, but the numbers are getting better. The trends are in the

Figure 1   **Number of African leaders by type**

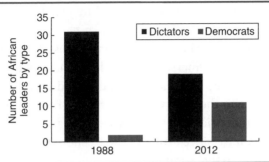

right direction. We have gone from 31 dictators to 19, if you want the exact numbers (see Figure 1). And we have gone from only two democracies in 1988 to 12 in 2012.

If you've been following the news just over the last few days,[2] Burkina Faso had a democratic election for the first time after decades of dictatorship.

People mistakenly think that economic freedom is something that benefits rich people. But, actually, as the Mubende and Ethiopia stories illustrate, the group that is really most vulnerable to having their property rights ignored is poor people.

Economic freedom which measures both the freedom of people to choose their own economic activities and property rights and other rights is something that has also been advancing recently. There is an independent group that ranks countries by economic freedom. Today, almost

---

2   Mid December 2015.

50 per cent of countries have an economic freedom rating as high as that which was enjoyed by just 10 per cent of countries in 1980.

Economic freedom is advancing across the globe. Instead of cocoa farmers, as used to happen in Ghana, being expropriated by governments that forced them to sell at a low price to the state with the produce being resold at a vastly higher price on world markets, those cocoa farmers in Ghana have since attained the freedom to sell at something close to the world price.

So, there are real new opportunities and choices for people in both the political sphere and in the economic sphere.

Of course, in Africa we have seen the best economic growth since independence, and probably in Africa's history. Since the mid 1990s, Africa has had very healthy economic growth.

Just to give you one specific hopeful sign, there are now today twice as many cell phone subscribers in Africa as there are in my home country, the US. This is not just teenagers talking to their girlfriends or boyfriends. This is farmers who are now able to find out what prices are and where they can get the best price; this is traders being able to know when supplies are available for them to buy and sell, and to feed hungry people. These cell phones are being used to make financial transfers and to make small bank loans.

These cell phones are, themselves, the creation of a generation of remarkable African entrepreneurs. Alieu Conteh, in the Democratic Republic of Congo, even in the middle of civil war, was creating cell phone towers on trees, stringing up the transmitters on the tops of trees and welding together scrap metal to make the cell phone towers.

In the midst of everything, the creativity and entrepreneurship of the African people, themselves, has created this remarkable success story.

Now, of course, there is still too much poverty, but the trends are in the right direction and the fastest progress against poverty is being made precisely because of the advance in political and economic freedom around the world. The same rights that were violated in Mubende, Uganda, and in the resettlement programme in Ethiopia are today being respected much more and this respect for rights is paying off much more.

What should we do to end poverty?

If you really insist on having me answer that question, 'What should we do to end poverty?' of course, the 'we' in that question was always part of the problem.

It was the assumption that we, the paternalistic, Western, condescending, pitying outsiders were going to be the source of the solutions, and, frankly, we are not as much a part of the solution as we think we are. That was the first problem with that question. Then, the second problem with that question is that we implicitly ignore the fact that one thing we should be focusing on is not making the rights of the poor worse in poor countries.

That includes, first of all, dismissing the technocratic illusion. Those of us who work in aid and development should drop the pretence of value-free analysis and politics-free analysis. We should openly join the battle of ideas on the side of freedom against dictatorship and advocate for the cause of freedom for the world's poor.

It also includes convincing our own fellow voters in the US and the UK that our own aid agencies should not violate the rights of the poor, our own foreign policy should not violate the rights of the poor, and our own military should not violate the rights of the poor. We should look at ourselves to see if we are complicit in violating the rights of the poor.

Freedom may be winning, but we know the battle is far from over. So it remains for all of us tonight to keep fighting for those ideals of freedom – for universal freedom for all. We need to convince many more that all people everywhere – women and men, black and white, rich and poor – deserve to be free at last.

2 QUESTIONS AND DISCUSSION[1]

SYLVIE ABOA-BRADWELL: I am Sylvie Aboa-Bradwell, Director of the Policy Centre for African Peoples. It is something that I created to fight against the dictatorship of foreign aid. I am also an entrepreneur.

Sir, I would like to congratulate you very much for framing this debate in terms of historical context, because, lest we forget, the cornerstone of the enslavement of Africans was that enslaving would help them by introducing them to civilisation and also to Christianity.

At the same time, in the same way that people were 'benefiting' from slavery centuries ago, right now, people are 'benefiting' in terms of – for the Bill Gateses of this world – having access to all types of powerful people.

Corrupt people in Africa are also 'benefiting' from this status quo, whereby there is absolutely no accountability and poor people are sustained by, really, the small amount of money given to them by so-called benefactors of the Save the Childrens of this world. My question is: In the same way that the anti-slavery campaigners really had something to

---

1   In editing this monograph, we have done our best to transcribe the names of those who asked questions from the audio recording.

campaign against, how can poor people organise in order to have a powerful voice against this aid orthodoxy?

JOHN STRAFFORD: Right now, in Paris, 40,000 people have assembled to try to get the developed nations to pay £100 bn a year to the undeveloped nations. Would you like to comment on that?

JOHN CHOWN: When communism collapsed and we decided that we wanted to help them become good capitalists, I was introduced to people in Brussels and I was introduced to people in various banks. I was horrified by the way in which aid and technical assistance was being organised.

I was then lucky enough to be found by the Know How Fund in the UK, which was a superb organisation that did everything in the right way.

Then, having all these things come back and seeing how much money was being wasted on bad projects, I was delighted to read a review of your book, which I bought and read with delight, and I found out that you knew exactly what needed doing.

Now, I've been fighting a battle since the last change of government, when the Labour government came in, to have the Know How Fund restored. Do you know about the Know How Fund, and would you be my ally in persuading people that this is the right way forward?

WILLIAM EASTERLY: It is true that, even during the times of slavery, the British and Americans, who have an amazing capacity for the self-justification of anything, made technocratic arguments at the time that slavery somehow made slaves better off.

It might have been true that, say, the diet of slaves was better than the diet of Africans who had not been captured into slavery. That obviously would not prove the technocratic case that slavery made slaves better off.

That is an even more extreme example of how you cannot ignore the question of consent and choice. 'Choice' has to be at the foundation of all of our discussion, and we cannot ignore our own complicity in the West. In the West, we so much want to talk about ourselves as aid agencies, as benefactors and as benevolent givers, and we are ignoring our own and our current history of supporting the oppression of poor people. As far as a movement is concerned, I think you are much better qualified than I am to lead that movement.

On the climate talks, I have to specialise a little bit, so I confess that is not an area I know as much about. Though I have noticed that the answers to the climate talks are equally technocratic and are equally dismissive in ignoring completely the actual choices and consent of all the people involved.

With regard to the last question, I am glad you mentioned the attempt to reform communism into capitalism. I have confessed to many sins tonight. I have to confess another one. I was involved in shock therapy in the former Soviet Union, which was still the Soviet Union when I first went there. Another guy named Jeff Sachs was also very involved. Both of us were wrong at the time.

Shock therapy was basically a short word for coercive advice by expert outsiders who think they know a lot more about your problems than you do. It did not work out well: the coercion did not work out well. Again, it's pretty much the same story that it was the technocratic mindset that, somehow, throwing off the shackles of communism involved just getting a lot of technical advice on how to run a capitalist system, a free economic system and a free political system.

One thing I remember was this: we literally had way too many Western economists who knew nothing about Russia, including me. Another group that I noticed a lot of in Moscow at the time were lawyers, advising them just how to rewrite the laws to look like Western laws, completely missing the point that the main drama going on was the battle of values of: 'Could a free system emerge after the long night of communism, totalitarianism, Stalin, Lenin and all the awful things that had gone before?'

That was the battle that was happening, and unfortunately, that battle was lost, partly because the West fumbled its own role so badly, precisely in this technocratic direction.

I don't know about the Know How Foundation, but I welcome everyone to check it out on your recommendation.

THERESA CARTHY: A lot of the literature I have read has said that the World Bank and other international institutions prefer technical solutions because they are very well prepared to implement those. Whereas, advocating for a certain political or social cause or helping to overthrow a dictatorship might be quite difficult for the World Bank. What is the role of the World Bank and other international institutions in your approach to development?

BEN: I think we would all agree that the examples you raised were clear violations of rights, but I struggle to see how the bulk of aid work constitutes a violation of rights. I think you have chosen some examples where it is very clear, and people in this room and people outside the room would agree that they represent violations of rights. But how does, for example, offering mosquito nets to people in Mozambique constitute a violation of rights? Is it not expanding their right to healthcare and, in turn, an education, for example?

I think you've picked some ridiculous examples to base your argument upon.

ALEX: You're against aid, but what about the new moves towards randomised trials, so things like credit banks and offering facilities to people that would ease constraints that are on them, so giving them more rights in a way? What do you think about that?

TOM: Do you think there is ever a tension between giving people more rights and not offering more technology? Can people have a right to technology that exists somewhere else in the world, if it's going to save their life or something like that?

WILLIAM EASTERLY: Let me answer both the question on the World Bank, 'What can the World Bank do about democracy?', and 'Are mosquito nets a violation of rights?'

For both those questions, of course, giving mosquito nets to a poor person does not violate their rights. If they say they want the mosquito net, you give them the mosquito net. That's fine. There is nothing wrong with that whatsoever.

When I said this was an accidental equilibrium, what is really happening is that the aid and development people feel like they must censor themselves, and the World Bank or Bill Gates cannot go into Ethiopia or Uganda holding up a big sign, saying, 'Overthrow the oppressive dictator'. Obviously, that is true, and I understand those political constraints. Indeed, not having mentioned that earlier might have been a bit unfair to Gates.

What is fair to say, however, is that Gates is also a huge voice and the World Bank is also a huge voice in the global debate on how development happens and should happen. You have a couple of actors – the World Bank and Gates – who censor themselves to never criticise dictators, to never talk about rights, to never talk about democracy, and they are participating in a global debate on how development happens.

I think this is very much a case that we can argue about, but I would argue that rights are the basic taproot foundation of development, and yet these actors are censoring their own participation in the debate by not even mentioning the rights of the poor.

That is what bothers me about this unintentional equilibrium in which we focus only on technical solutions. We are not allowed to talk about democracy and about rights. That's the unintentional equilibrium. The World Bank literally put into its own charter that it can never discuss political systems. It was put in way back in 1944, and it has actually violated that principle many times since then.

In a recent World Development Report, it even seemed in favour of outside military intervention in poor countries, which sounds pretty much to me like an interference in local political systems.

How can we have an organisation be such a big voice in the world of development ideas that is not allowed to talk about democracy? That is ridiculous. That's counter-productive in the battle of ideas.

The battle of ideas – what I'm arguing – is ultimately more important in determining the fate of these technical solutions than just the mere fact of whether one aid agency at one moment in time is handing out a mosquito net.

JAMES SPROULE: What led to your epiphany and why is your epiphany still so rare?

DAVID SHIPLEY: To what extent do you think that aid given to dictatorships retards or accelerates the transition from dictatorship to democracy?

JAMES ROBERTS: Should we leave people to overthrow their own dictators or should we at least pencil in, as some part of an action plan, some means of helping? If so, what could the outside world do?

WILLIAM EASTERLY: I am not sure I would have used the word 'epiphany'.

Again, I want to be clear. This is not some kind of self-righteous crusade by those of us who argue for rights and for moral norms in development. I really do respect those who have the opposite view. They could be right. I could be wrong. The important thing is just that the debate should happen.

I guess the only thing I would say is that the Mubende, Uganda, example, itself, had some effect because I was monitoring it in real time as it was happening. It was very disillusioning, frankly, to see how little reaction there was in the aid and development world.

I was writing a blog at the time called 'Aid Watch' – and we can monitor our traffic numbers, day-to-day, as we all do – and I noticed that any discussion of Mubende, Uganda, and rights violations by the World Bank just sent our traffic numbers heading south, as if nobody really cared.

Then, I decided to write a book – for which, apparently, there is no audience whatsoever – on the same subject, and that was the epiphany.

The first problem with aid to dictators is really in the realm of ideas: that by giving aid to dictators, we are affirming that we think the dictators are part of the solution instead of the reality that they're really part of the problem.

The second problem with aid to dictators is that it arguably makes them more likely to last longer: they have more money from outside support, and can ignore more domestic factors because they have more outside money supporting them.

I was happy to see the recent Nobel Laureate, Angus Deaton, someone I admire a lot, make the same argument much more forcefully and much more eloquently in his book *The Great Escape*, that aid to dictators is just making things worse rather than better.

On the last question – 'How could we, sympathisers in the West, help poor people, Africans or whoever we're talking about get rid of their own dictators?' – let's take one thing off the table right away. I think in almost all cases, it's a really dumb idea to use our own military intervention to get rid of a dictator.

I think it is a fairly self-contradictory idea, frankly. It is like saying: 'We are going to coerce you to have the right to be uncoerced. Enjoy it.' It doesn't make sense. It's just not the way that freedom travels. It doesn't travel at the point of a gun.

What I have noticed in my own interactions with people around the world, fighting for democratic rights in poor countries, is just talking to, for example, members of the Ethiopian diaspora I have met on many occasions, they indeed actually do feel really discouraged when they see Western aid agencies supporting the dictator who is oppressing them.

They feel some kind of moral support and encouragement when there are some voices that are supporting them or protesting against the jailing of a peaceful Ethiopian dissident named Eskinder Nega, who is just a peaceful blogger, or in support of the more recent Zone 9 bloggers who were imprisoned, or against the denial of US and UK finance and food aid to opposition supporters in Ethiopia.

Protesting these rights violations is encouraging and helpful, and there can be a community of moral support that makes freedom more likely to happen, but never are outsiders going to be in the lead. I think the fight for freedom is always going to be, first and foremost, a homegrown effort of people fighting for their own rights.

TOM PAPWORTH: You have made a compelling case that the solutions to developing world poverty need to come from within the developing world, and you have cast doubt on the ability of developed-world technocrats to offer solutions. What role, if any, is there for overseas aid?

ANON (FEMALE): You have made the case for people fighting for their own freedom from within the country. To what extent would you say education is really the answer to this and that you can empower people with liberal minds to help kick-start self-sufficiency rather than having to rely on organisations such as the World Bank, which often give loans with strings attached?

It would also help them understand the importance of democracy and human rights, and thereby challenge their autocrats for these rights and hopefully overthrow them.

SAM JORDAN: As far as measuring development goes, what is your opinion on using Sen's 'capabilities approach' versus using more traditional means like GDP per capita?

WILLIAM EASTERLY: The first question is 'What role for aid agencies?' and the second is about education as a great way of supporting home-grown efforts. I think the second question helps me answer the first one.

There can be a role for aid, never working through any oppressive dictator, but always thinking: 'How can there be some sorts of people-to-people transfers in which we're supporting people in their own home-grown efforts for further development or to further freedom?'

I think education is a great example of that. I would give one very specific example. I am not suggesting it is the only possible vehicle, but it is a good example: simply giving scholarships and making available widespread scholarship programmes. This has been done at different times with very positive effects for students from poor countries to either study in their own countries or study in Western countries.

That has the properties that a less paternalistic and a more rights-driven approach could have because you are giving a scholarship to a student who is in charge of their own studies, in charge of their own life, deciding how best they are going to develop themselves through education, and all you are doing is making that education possible with a scholarship.

That is a small micro example. Indeed, there are many ways that can be found to support many home-grown efforts, but the important thing that has to happen is that the home-grown efforts have to be at the centre and in the lead.

In the development universe, we spend a lot of time watching the debates of a lot of middle-aged white male professors arguing with each other, and they are at the centre, including me. We should not be at the centre. We should have a Copernican revolution, where we hear a lot less from those people, including me, and we hear a lot more from the home-grown efforts of poor people themselves, and we're talking a lot more about how we can support what they are already doing and not our brilliant ideas for what we think they should do.

On Sen, I think the 'capabilities approach' was a valuable addition to thinking about development more broadly, but, actually, I would like to mention Sen in another context.

He deserves a lot of honour and recognition as one of the first to really bring up the idea of freedom in his great book, *Development as Freedom*; to raise the point that freedom was central to how development happens and that ability to choose and to consent is central to how development should happen in a morally consistent way.

He also has this very arresting and persuasive argument that democracies do not have famines. He is well known for that argument, which is another example of how democratic accountability is more powerful than all the technical solutions that we have ever come up with of food shipments and malnutrition capsules to confront famine.

Democracies do not have famines; drought-prone Botswana has never had a famine in its record of independent democratic rule; autocratic Ethiopia has had one famine after another.

Sen deserves a lot of credit for being one of the first to identify that as the core of the problem.

DOMINIC: You haven't touched on something which seems to have gripped, as you say, the technocrats for decades, which is population control or birth control. The solution to allegedly starving Africans was to eliminate them. In China, of course, the UN Population Agency backed the Chinese government, and we see the results now. How much of this came out of what we might call the 'aid community'? How much responsibility rests there, and do you have any observations on that?

EDDIE LLOYD: Mr Easterly, it sounds as if the proponents of a more technical policy are right in their diagnosis but wrong in the provision of their cure. If, as you say, economic freedom is so involved in this cure, what, over the past 30 or so years, have been the most effective measures in bringing about those extended freedoms?

CONSTANTINE: My question concerns China, mainly. That doesn't really go into the aid question much, but you made a very compelling argument, I think, about how economic freedoms and democratic freedoms in the end lead to development. If you look at the largest development miracle, to some extent, in the past 20 years, it is probably China, which lifted 300 million people out of poverty. I would probably argue that China is not really a relatively free country. Rather, people feel a lot of oppression, I think, in China, and generally the state is quite involved with oppressive measures.

I was wondering what your take was on that and how that fits in with your larger idea that academic and democratic freedoms lead to poverty reduction.

PHILIP BOOTH: You criticise Bill Gates, so your argument is not that, on the one hand, private is good and that, on the other hand, state is bad. It is a different type of argument. You have also indicated what types of programmes might be helpful that could be initiated by the state. If you were somebody who had some money to donate to a charity, what are the characteristics of a charitable programme which you would see as desirable in aiding development?

WILLIAM EASTERLY: Well, Philip, as someone who tries to specialise, I certainly am not going to be in the business of recommending individual charities. I think we're talking about principles here. One of the principles that I am trying to argue for is that we already have lots of attempts at direct technical solutions and we have too little advocacy. So I think one vastly underutilised area of development is advocacy for more freedom for poor people, for more political and economic rights, and for more human rights for poor people. There are some NGOs that are doing that: Human Rights Watch, Amnesty International, Freedom House in the US, and there are probably some I am not aware of in the UK.

This advocacy, as I was trying to argue, is itself a powerful force for social change. You are changing the norms that govern the technical solutions that will, in the long run, happen.

And now, the two questions on China: the high economic growth under what are obviously dictators in China, and the one-child policy for population control. The first is more of a technical discussion, so forgive this wonky answer.

Why do we get excited about China? It is not because of its level of per capita income. The level of per capita income will increase with economic freedom and political freedom – a high level of freedom predicts a high level of long-run, sustained prosperity. Deprivation and oppression predict poverty. It is a level prediction.

Then, what follows from that level prediction is a changes prediction. And this gets to the question of, 'What is the most effective means to engineer development?' If you get some kind of usually home-grown effort to increase freedom, what you expect to respond is economic growth. There will be a rise in the level of income from a rise in the level of freedom – this change in levels of income is growth.

I think a better description of the China miracle is that there actually was a big increase in freedom in China. After Mao, there was a vast increase in economic freedom. There was a vast increase in personal freedom of Chinese citizens, including many that I have as my students at NYU, to travel and to determine their own destinies compared with the oppression and totalitarian control under Mao.

Obviously, not much changed in terms of formal political freedom, but, even there, the dictators now are certainly not as bad as Mao, who is down in the history books with tens of millions of deaths from the Great Famine, the Great Leap Forward and the Cultural Revolution.

As horrific as things still are in the Chinese political system, there is still the positive change in freedom that goes with this unleashing of the remarkable energies of the Chinese people.

I think part of that story is also the remarkable energies of the overseas Chinese outside China and outside the control of the Chinese government who have invested vast amounts back into China once the economy was liberalised.

Then, lastly, to close tonight, on the grim subject of population control and the one-child policy in China – it is shocking to me now. It was not as shocking to me as it should have been earlier in my career that development economists really were so tolerant of really incredibly abusive, coercive mechanisms such as the one-child policy in China as a means of population control.

It is very much a debatable subject that there is some outside need to force poor people to have fewer children. If there is some environmental reason, for example, why population growth is too fast, then at least you should use voluntary programmes to persuade people to have fewer children.

The one-child policy is just such a shocking violation, and it is not the only one. Actually, population control was one of the areas where there were coercive policies, such as the forced sterilisation, under Indira Gandhi in India. And there are many other examples sponsored by Western foundations and by Western aid agencies. They are documented very well in the book *Fatal Misconception* by Matthew Connelly (2008).

Again, it just shows how much the development mindset has been so paternalistic that it would tolerate such a shocking violation of such a private decision of poor people, of whether they can have another child or whether their child should be male or female. This is such a shocking intrusion into the most basic rights of poor people, and shocking that it was tolerated for so long in the development community.

Today, it is now being ended by China, but it is still not receiving anywhere near the sort of historical retrospection that it deserves. That is an example of how badly we do indeed need, tonight, to close on this note: the importance of the simple cause of advocacy of equal rights for the world's poor.

3 WILLIAM EASTERLY'S POLITICAL ECONOMY OF INTERVENTION

A commentary on William Easterly's lecture

Abigail R. Hall-Blanco

Introduction

Why are some nations rich and others poor? This question has concerned economists since the beginning of the profession. Adam Smith brought the question to life in *The Wealth of Nations*. Over time, the field of economics has changed dramatically. From the 'marginal revolution' of Menger, Jevons and Walras, to the rise of Keynesianism, to the introduction of econometric models, game theory and randomised control trials, Smith would be surprised to see the way many modern economists conduct their research. But he would be not be surprised to see the continued salience of his concerns.

Since Smith wrote, economists have done substantial work on economic development. They have added many new questions to the development puzzle. For example, why is it that, in spite of years of planning and billions of dollars spent on countless programmes, we have been unable to systematically induce economic development?

Although technology and advances in agriculture, medicine and communications have improved the lives of billions, poverty remains a real problem. Today, nearly a billion people continue to live on less than $2.00 per day (World Bank 2016b).

How is it that, despite the best-laid plans of economists and other experts, and the well-intentioned policies of countless do-gooders, many proposed solutions for economic development have failed? This is the fundamental issue William Easterly looks to address in his Hayek lecture. It is a central theme throughout his prolific and influential body of work (see Easterly 2001, 2006a,b, 2008, 2011, 2009, 2014; Easterly and Williamson 2011; Easterly and Pfutze 2008).

In order to address this question, Easterly highlights what he sees as the main problems with modern development initiatives. Easterly posits that, over the past several decades, most of those working on the economics of development have thought of poverty as a technical problem with technical solutions. He notes that many problems afflicting developing countries seem to have simple solutions. Vitamin A deficiency, for example, can be cured with cheap supplements. What about malaria? That can be easily combated with chemicals or bed nets. Clean water can often be found by drilling a new well. He goes on to say, however, that while solutions to these problems appear straightforward and easily implemented, these problems continue to persist despite decades of efforts.

These are not the only examples of 'simple' poverty solutions failing to achieve desired goals. In his 2001 work,

The Elusive Quest for Growth: Economists' Adventures and Misadventures in the Tropics, Easterly highlights many development plans formulated by international institutions such as the World Bank and the International Monetary Fund (IMF). Once hailed as the harbingers of progress, these programmes have not only failed to bring about progress, but in some cases have made conditions for the world's poorest even worse.

The history of development economics contains a variety of examples of these panaceas that failed. In *The Elusive Quest,* for example, Easterly examines at length policies directed towards investment in physical capital. These approaches, based on the Harrod–Domar model, maintain that investment spending is the driver of economic growth (Easterly 2001: 28–31). For years, Western development agencies sought to fill the 'finance gaps' of less-developed countries (LDCs) in order to obtain desired growth rates as suggested by the models. Easterly reminds us, however, that these policies did not increase growth or investment or lead to development. The same story can be repeated over and over for aid programmes dedicated to increasing educational attainment, improving healthcare, supporting population control and debt forgiveness. Policies intended to 'fix' problems surrounding politics, geography and natural resource issues have likewise been tried with little success. Easterly argues further that many in development agencies almost completely ignore the institutional structures in which development programmes are conceptualised and implemented. By ignoring the incentives faced by aid givers, aid recipients and others, says

Easterly, it should come as no surprise that many development policies have failed to achieve their desired outcomes.

The influence of Easterly's work in development economics cannot be overstated. Without a doubt, his criticisms of the IMF, the World Bank and the general approach to economic development have prompted many in economics and other disciplines to focus a much-needed critical eye on development policy. But his critiques of 'technical solutions' and the neglect of institutions and incentives encompass topics outside of development economics. In fact, the points he raises are valid in *all* types of government intervention. The purposes of this chapter are to discuss the theoretical underpinnings of Easterly's critique, and to show how they apply to other important interventions. First, I argue that Easterly's ideas are intimately connected with those of two Nobel laureates, F. A. Hayek and James M. Buchanan. Taken together, their ideas illustrate how plans for economic development are likely to fail. Second, I discuss how these same critiques may be applied more broadly to any top-down intervention and provide specific examples from military episodes.

Hayek, the knowledge problem and economic calculation

To understand the failure of many development projects, we need a deeper consideration of top-down planning in general. In particular, this calls for an appreciation of economic calculation. The first fundamental principle of economics is scarcity. Put simply, people want more goods and services than are readily available. It follows from this that people must make choices about how resources will be used and economic calculation is necessary in order to solve the problem of how to allocate them. Ludwig von Mises (1922, 1927, 1944, 1949) explained why top-down economic calculation under socialism was impossible. He further explained how attempts at central planning would ultimately result in costly failure. Boettke (2001: 31) offers a clear summary of Mises's argument:

> Without private property in the means of production, there will be no market ... Without a market ... there will be no monetary prices ... Without monetary prices ... economic decision-makers will be unable to rationally calculate the alternative use of capital goods.

It follows from Mises's work that the market process, with its system of private property, prices that reflect relative scarcities and signals of profit and loss, not only encourages entrepreneurial activity, but works to correct calculation errors. Taken together, these mechanisms drive resources to their highest-valued use.

Following Mises, Hayek argued that constructing rational economic order through central planning by an individual or group of individuals was impossible. Economic coordination and planning, he pointed out (1945: 80; 1968), require the knowledge of many individuals with precise information of 'time and space.' This information, dispersed among countless individual actors, can only be brought together via entrepreneurial discovery and the competitive process of the market. Such interactions, therefore, are necessary for economic calculation (see Hayek 1945; Kirzner 1978: 8–11, 1985, 1997). It follows for Hayek that no central planners could *ever* acquire the needed information to engage in effective economic calculation, as they would lack a comparable mechanism that can mimic the discovery process of the market.

Mises and Hayek were working to address the arguments around socialism in inter-war and mid-twentieth-century Europe, but the same type of reasoning can be applied to explain the failure of many more recent governments and development organisations to achieve development and sustained economic growth. They lack the necessary knowledge to allocate scarce resources to their highest-valued use. Easterly makes a similar argument in *The White Man's Burden* when he discusses the difference between 'planners' and 'searchers.' A planner, according to Easterly, 'thinks he already knows the answers.' A searcher, by contrast, 'admits he doesn't know the answers in advance; he believes that poverty is a complicated triangle of political, social, historical, institutional and technological factors' (Easterly 2006: 6).

Many economists and other development experts are clearly best described as 'planners' in this sense. The dominant narrative in current development agencies is that enlightened experts can design reforms and other programmes to fix development problems. Just as Hayek and Mises warned, this planning has often resulted in failure. While experts may have a general idea of what conditions are necessary for economic development, they lack the knowledge of how to develop these conditions where they are not already present. There are a variety of examples of this 'knowledge problem' in development and foreign aid. Christopher Coyne (2013: 90) highlights many such cases as they relate to humanitarian aid. In one recent instance, Médecins Sans Frontiéres (MSF, Doctors without Borders) reported that hospital and other medical equipment donated to Afghan hospitals was simply 'piling up' (Coyne 2013: 90). While experts knew that people in the region needed medical assistance, they failed to recognise that many Afghan medical personnel wouldn't know how to use the equipment, much less be able to make repairs. The report stated, 'This equipment is usually dropped off with little explanation and no anticipation of maintenance; most of it sits in boxes, collecting dust, unopened and unused' (Doctors Without Borders 2010: 2). In another case, a study of medications donated to Indonesia following a tsunami found that 70 per cent of medication labels were in foreign languages – meaning healthcare workers were unable to read them. Some 60 per cent of the medicines sent were not relevant for tsunami victims, and healthcare workers were forced to give up precious space for storage (Coyne 2013: 90–91).

Many argue that those engaged in development projects, and planning more generally, have developed feedback systems which allow them to adapt to changing conditions. Such organisations as the World Bank and IMF have implemented reforms at various points to address problems and supposedly improve performance. For example, the World Bank has used reviews conducted by the Independent Evaluation Group (IEG) since the 1970s to evaluate more than 11,000 projects (World Bank 2016a). The agency likewise obtains feedback through annual reviews, corporate evaluations and global programme reviews (Independent Evaluation Group 2014). The idea is that, by using such reviews to evaluate their projects, the organisation can, through a process of trial and error, work to allocate resources effectively. Easterly (2001: 5), however, points to a variety of weaknesses of this feedback system, observing that 'it is very hard for aid bureaucracies to get constructive feedback from past mistakes ... any admission of past failure is a threat to getting new aid resources to dispense in the future.'

In spite of access to extensive data on their projects, immense financial resources and these feedback mechanisms, organisations such as the World Bank continue to lack essential knowledge of what projects ought to be implemented, where to implement them and what projects will ultimately be likely to be successful. Numerous studies have pointed out myriad problems with the World Bank's programmes and feedback mechanisms. To give but one example, consider a 1996 study which found that of the 66 developing countries receiving aid from the World Bank for more than 25 years, 37 were no better off than before they received the aid. In fact, 20 countries were *worse* off (Johnson 1996). Some countries saw positively dismal results. Niger and Nicaragua, for example, received more than $589 million and $637 million, respectively, in aid from the World Bank between 1965 and 1995. In that period, GDP in both countries shrank by more than 50 per cent (ibid.).

In a market context, questions of what projects to undertake, where and how to implement them would be answered via profit and loss. Positive profits would indicate that a project was effective and entrepreneurs would continue that activity. A negative profit – a loss – would indicate that resources would be better used elsewhere. Without these mechanisms and entrepreneurial actions to guide them, development agencies and governments are consistently unable to determine which projects will be successful and which will fail. Unable to engage in rational economic calculation, they support projects that ultimately fail to meet their goals.

Buchanan, public choice and development

In addition to the hurdles presented by the inability of development experts to engage in rational economic calculation, there are other problems preventing development experts, organisations and other groups from consistently 'picking winners' when it comes to development projects. In order to understand these problems, we need to reference the economics of bureaucracy, the organisational structure of many development agencies (e.g. the IMF and the World Bank), governments, non-government organisations (NGOs) and non-profit organisations (NPOs).

Work on the economics of bureaucracy finds that, without profit and loss signals to indicate success or failure, bureaucratic agencies gauge achievement differently. In particular, bureaucracies measure success by the size of their discretionary budgets and the number of subordinate agents

(Niskanen 1971, 1975; Migué and Bélanger 1974). As opposed to competing in the marketplace for profit, bureaucracies instead vie against other agencies for government resources.

This dynamic implies that bureaucracies will engage in intense rent-seeking behaviour in an effort to increase their budgets and expand their personnel. The logic is straightforward. If an agency demonstrates to the larger government that some of their programmes are successful, they can then claim they would be able to achieve still greater results with more resources. Even if an agency cannot produce any positive reports, it can still use such data to solicit greater government support. Failures can easily be blamed, not on poor planning or execution, but on a lack of resources.

This rent-seeking behaviour has additional implications for how development agencies allocate resources. Without profit and loss signals to serve as a guide, projects are designed, implemented and funded by following a predetermined set of rules (Mises 1944: 50). Unlike the situation in a market, where entrepreneurs can quickly adapt to new information and changing conditions, making changes in a bureaucracy is much more difficult. In addition, the absence of the profit signal means that there is little incentive to please 'customers' in development projects. Instead, agents attempt to please bureaucratic superiors. This means that those in the best position to say what is needed – those receiving the aid – are often left unheard. Taken together, this implies that resources are more likely to be allocated not to those most in need or in a position to best use the resources, but to those with a comparative advantage in rent-seeking.

Many individuals tend to neglect these ideas when discussing non-profits, development agencies and governments more generally. They assume that these groups of actors work exclusively in the 'public interest'. That is, those responsible for development projects set aside private incentives and their own self-interest in order to construct policies and programmes that serve the public as a whole as opposed to particular groups.

James M. Buchanan, however, noted that a public interest framework ignores the bureaucratic context in which government and other agencies operate. As Buchanan (2003), Brennan and Buchanan (1985), Buchanan and Tullock (1962), Tullock (2005) and others have argued, failing to extend the behavioural assumptions of rational self-interest across all contexts leads to a poor understanding of policy. While not denying that bureaucratic actors may value the wellbeing of others, these authors point out that those in positions to influence the trajectory of policy do not look solely to maximise the welfare of others. Instead, they suggest, just like private actors, they respond to the incentives created by the institutions, or 'rules of the game' in which they operate (see Buchanan 2003; North 1990). It follows that policies serving the public interest will only be pursued to the extent they overlap with bureaucratic interests. This 'public choice' framework, assuming that public actors respond to incentives, applies to any kind of political activity, development projects included.

Easterly echoes many of Buchanan's points throughout his body of work. Time and again he discusses the incentives faced by those working in bureaucratic development agencies (see Easterly 2006, 2014). He points out that the incentives faced by many individuals in development agencies lead them to pursue projects which align with their own self-interest as opposed to the interests of their 'customers'. He points out that many potentially worthwhile projects are less likely to be pursued because of the institutional structure of development agencies. With the economics of bureaucracy looming large in the background, potentially effective projects are scrapped. In order to show that their projects are successful, bureaucratic agents pursue projects for which they can clearly define an output (e.g. money dispensed as opposed to services delivered). He likewise discusses how the incentives facing aid agencies induce the production of many 'low-return' outputs and few 'high-return' outputs. For example, development agencies are more likely to produce reports and 'frameworks' for evaluating or developing new projects as opposed to engaging in critical ex post evaluation of previous ventures. Moreover, he discusses how the incentives facing development agencies lead them actively to obscure results of their efforts (Easterly 2002). Others have made similar critiques of development projects, employing Buchanan's public choice framework (see Coyne 2013; Hall 2014; Mathers 2012).

Easterly's critique and the example of military intervention

Taken together, the knowledge problems discerned by Mises and Hayek, and the issue of incentives raised by

Buchanan, make a powerful argument for scepticism regarding development planning. Throughout his body of work, Easterly frequently returns to these ideas to explain why grand plans for economic development have consistently failed.

While these insights are useful in explaining the failures of economic development programmes, similar reasoning may be applied to any sort of top-down intervention. Military interventions, or the preparations for possible military activities, provide countless examples of how knowledge and incentive problems lead to policy failure as well as a variety of unintended consequences. Just as with development agencies, governments lack the capacity to engage in projects such as 'nation building', 'the war on terror' and 'spreading democracy'. Easterly (2006b: 312) makes this point in *White Man's Burden*, saying, 'military intervention is too perfect an example of what ... you should *not* do ... The military is even more insulated from the interests of the poor than aid agencies are.' He dedicates an entire chapter to discussing how military intervention and development have become inextricably linked, making military activity a logical place to apply Easterly's critiques.

First, consider a variation of the knowledge problems discussed by Hayek. Just as the 'planners' of development projects tend to ignore the limitations of their knowledge, so too do those who advocate military intervention. It is impossible for policymakers to obtain, let alone process, all the information necessary to determine whether or not an intervention will be successful. Moreover, as a result of their lack of knowledge, they are unable to anticipate all the consequences of activities abroad (see Duncan and Coyne 2015).

The consequences can be severe. Take, for example, the case of Libya. In 2011, the Obama administration successfully implemented and enforced a no-fly zone over the country and the country's long-time dictator, Muammar Gaddafi, was killed. Initially, this was hailed as a victory by coalition forces. But leaders failed to understand how such an intervention would impact on the country and the surrounding area. As a result of their knowledge failure, Gaddafi's overthrow led to a power vacuum in the country and a civil war erupted. Not only did grand plans to bring democracy to the state fail, but the war continues to have substantial impacts on Libyan citizens and the broader region (see Coyne 2014). In fact, a plurality of Libyans state they are worse off now than under the previous regime (Interventions Watch 2014). Similar knowledge failures can be observed in other interventions such as those in Afghanistan, Iraq and Somalia. In each case, failure to understand the intricate social, political and other frameworks led to complete failure (see Coyne 2008; Leeson 2007).

The public choice framework Easterly applies to problems in economic development is also directly applicable to cases of military intervention. Just as policymakers, the public and many scholars believe development organisations are purely interested in the public good, similar assumptions are made regarding foreign military intervention. However, numerous examples show such assumptions fail to describe actual policy. Hall (2015) and Hall and Coyne (2014), for example, found that the failure to appreciate the incentives facing policymakers has led to a rapid increase in the use of drones in US foreign interventions, despite data indicating that the technology may fail to meet a variety of policy objectives. The same authors find that arms sales conducted by the US government fall prey to both knowledge and incentive problems. As a result, the global arms market is subject to rampant system effects, principal–agent problems, rent-seeking and an increase in the overall amount of global arms (Coyne and Hall 2014). Coyne et al. (2016) find that drug interdiction policies in Afghanistan have actually undermined many of the goals of the war on terror. Failing to understand the complex social and political landscape of the country, the US government implemented policies that not only failed to decrease opium poppy production, but also strengthened the Taliban.

Conclusion

Taken together, the critiques laid out by Hayek and Buchanan, and utilised by Easterly, are just as relevant to issues of military intervention as to issues of development. In both cases, individuals or groups of individuals attempt to impose top-down solutions in order to address very complex problems. In both cases, however, we see both knowledge and incentive problems. Planners, lacking the ability to know and interpret all the necessary information, impose relatively simple plans on dynamic and complex societies. Negative consequences follow. Similarly, we see that both military interventions and development projects are subjected to public choice problems. Just as any other economic actor responds to the incentives he or she faces, so too do individuals involved in military operations and development activities. In both cases, perverse incentives lead, at a minimum, to wasted resources and poor resource allocation.

If we take these critiques seriously, it follows that we should be sceptical of a variety of interventions. Problems of limited knowledge and perverse incentives mean that policies designed to produce specific outcomes will be limited in their effectiveness. As Easterly and others have demonstrated, these activities often not only fail to meet their desired objectives, but generate a variety of unintended and undesirable consequences.

The next natural question is, what can be done? If top-down plans are likely to fail, what then are the alternatives? Here, again, we may make an important distinction between 'unblocking reforms' and 'end-state reforms'. End-state reforms, currently implemented by both development groups and advocates of military intervention, are those that seek to change or achieve certain predefined outcomes. These types of reforms fall prey to the critiques raised by Hayek and Buchanan. Unblocking reforms, however, seek to remove barriers to discovery, allowing individuals to better engage in the discovery process. These reforms do not look to achieve a particular outcome, but work to create an environment in which individuals may engage in peaceful discovery. They allow market forces, incentives, and profit and loss to drive societies to better outcomes.

At the least, these critiques suggest a need for humility when discussing any kind of 'grand plan'. As Easterly states, 'it is much easier to describe the problems facing poor countries than it is to come up with workable solutions to their poverty' (Easterly 2001: 291). In a similar way, those advocating military intervention for purposes both noble and ignoble should observe similar humility.

References

Boettke, P. J. (2001) *Calculus and Coordination: Essays on Socialism and Transitional Political Economy.* New York: Routledge.

Brennan, G. and Buchanan, J. M. (1985) *The Reason of Rules: Constitutional Political Economy.* Cambridge University Press.

Buchanan, J. M. (2003) Public choice: politics without romance. *Policy* 19(3): 13–18.

Buchanan, J. M. and Tullock, G. (1962) *The Calculus of Consent: Logical Foundations of Constitutional Democracy.* Ann Arbor, MI: University of Michigan Press.

Coyne, C. J. (2008) *After War: The Political Economy of Exporting Democracy.* Stanford, CA: Stanford University Press.

Coyne, C. J. (2013) *Doing Bad by Doing Good: Why Humanitarian Action Fails.* Stanford, CA: Stanford University Press.

Coyne, C. J. (2014) Foreign intervention: a case for humility. Dinner Address to the IHS Board of Directors in Honor of Jerry Fullinwider's Retirement from the Board. Available at http://www.ccoyne.com/Foreign_Intervention_-_A_Case_for_Humility.pdf (accessed 11 April 2016).

Coyne, C. J. and Hall, A. R. (2014) The case against U.S. arms monopoly. *Atlantic Economic Journal* 42(2): 83–100.

Coyne, C. J., Hall-Blanco, A. R. and Burns, S. (2016) The war on drugs in Afghanistan: another failed experiment in interdiction. *The Independent Review*, pp. 95–119.

Doctors Without Borders (2010) Afghanistan: a return to humanitarian action. Available at http://www.doctorswithoutbord ers.org/news-stories/special-report/afghanistan-return-hu manitarian-action (accessed 24 March 2016).

Duncan, T. K. and Coyne, C. J. (2015) The political economy of foreign intervention. In *Oxford Handbook of Austrian Economics* (ed. P. J. Boettke and C. J. Coyne). Oxford University Press.

Easterly, W. (2001) *The Elusive Quest for Growth: Economists' Adventures and Misadventures in the Tropics*. Cambridge, MA: MIT Press.

Easterly, W. (2002) The cartel of good intentions: the problem of bureaucracy in foreign aid. *Journal of Policy Reform* 5(4): 223–50.

Easterly, W. (2006a) Planners vs. searchers in foreign aid. *Asian Development Review* 23(2): 1–35.

Easterly, W. (2006b) *The White Man's Burden: Why the West's Efforts to Aid the Rest Have Done So Much Ill and So Little Good*. New York: Penguin Press.

Easterly, W. (2008) Institutions: top down or bottom up? *American Economic Review* 92(2): 95–99.

Easterly, W. (2009) Can the West save Africa? *Journal of Economic Literature* 47(2): 373–447.

Easterly, W. (2014) *The Tyranny of Experts: Economists, Dictators, and the Forgotten Rights of the Poor*. New York: Basic Books.

Easterly, W. and Pfutze, T. (2008) Where does the money go? Best and worst practices in foreign aid. *Journal of Economic Perspectives* 22(2): 29–52.

Easterly, W. and Williamson, C. (2011) Rhetoric versus reality: the best and worst of aid agency practices. *World Development* 39(11): 1930–49.

Hall, A. R. (2014) Mountains of disappointment: the failure of state-led development in Appalachia. *Journal of Private Enterprise* 19(2): 165–89.

Hall, A. R. (2015) Drones: public interest, public choice, and the expansion of unmanned aerial vehicles. *Peace Economics, Peace Science, and Public Policy* 21(2): 273–300.

Hall, A. R. and Coyne, C. J. (2014) The political economy of drones. *Defence and Peace Economics* 27(4): 273–300.

Hayek, F. A. (1945) The use of knowledge in society. In *Individualism and Economic Order*. University of Chicago Press.

Hayek, F. A. [1968] (2002) Competition as a discovery procedure. *Quarterly Journal of Austrian Economics* 5(3): 9–23.

Independent Evaluation Group (2014) *Evaluations*. Available at http://ieg.worldbank.org/webpage/evaluations (accessed 17 March 2016)

Interventions Watch (2014) Plurality of Libyans continue to think they're worse off now than under Gadaffi, 13 March. Available at https://interventionswatch.wordpress.com/2014/03/13/plurality-of-libyans-continue-to-think-theyre-worse-of-now-than-under-gadaffi/ (accessed 17 March 2016).

Johnson, B. T. (1996) The World Bank and economic growth: 50 years of failure. Heritage Foundation. Available at http://www.heritage.org/research/reports/1996/05/bg1082nbsp-the-world-bank-and-economic-growth (accessed 17 March 2016).

Kirzner, I. (1978) *Competition and Entrepreneurship*. University of Chicago Press.

Kirzner, I. (1985) *Discovery and the Capitalist Process.* University of Chicago Press.

Kirzner, I. (1997) Entrepreneurial discovery and the competitive market process: an Austrian approach. *Journal of Economic Literature* 35(1): 60–85.

Leeson, P. T. (2007) Better off stateless: Somalia before and after government collapse. *Journal of Comparative Economics* 35(4): 689–710.

Mathers, R. L. (2012) The failure of state-led economic development on American Indian reservations. *The Independent Review* 17(2): 65–80.

Migué, J.-L. and Bélanger, G. (1974) Toward a general theory of managerial discretion. *Public Choice* 28: 24–28.

Mises, L. von [1920] (1990) *Economic Calculation in the Socialist Commonwealth.* Auburn: Ludwig von Mises Institute.

Mises, L. von [1922] (1981) *Socialism: An Economic and Sociological Analysis.* Indianapolis: Liberty Classics.

Mises, L. von [1927] (2005) *Liberalism: The Classical Tradition.* Indianapolis: Liberty Fund.

Mises, L. von [1944] (1983) *Bureaucracy.* Grove City: The Libertarian Press.

Mises, L. von [1949] (1998) *Human Action: A Treatise on Economics* (scholar's edition). Auburn: Ludwig von Mises Institute.

Niskanen Jr, W. N. (1971) *Bureaucracy and Representative Government.* Chicago and New York City: Aldine, Atherton.

Niskanen Jr, W. N. (1975) Bureaucrats and politicians. *Journal of Law and Economics* 18(3): 617–43.

Tullock, G. (2005) (1965) *Bureaucracy.* Indianapolis: Liberty Fund.

World Bank (2016a) IEG World Bank project performance rat-
     ings. Available at http://data.worldbank.org/data-catalog/I
     EG (accessed 17 March 2016).

World Bank (2016b) Poverty: overview. Available at http://www
     .worldbank.org/en/topic/poverty/overview (accessed 17
     March 2016).

4 WILLIAM EASTERLY'S CHALLENGE TO THE DEVELOPMENT COMMUNITY

A commentary on William Easterly's lecture

Christian Bjørnskov

Introduction

William Easterly is not only widely known as one of the world's most eminent development economists, but also as a forceful opponent of the way in which the West tries to promote growth in developing countries. In particular, Easterly has characterised the way foreign aid is designed and projects are implemented as a 'tyranny of experts'.

In his Hayek lecture, Easterly continues to expound his critique of the way most donors and practitioners think about development. His main argument, backed by several telling examples, is that the rights, opinions and insights of poor people are ignored. Instead, donor agencies and the development community in general view problems and challenges in developing countries as purely technical problems. They therefore call for technical solutions that are much easier to implement with the help of dictatorial regimes and with disregard for the rights of ordinary people in the developing world.

Although Easterly's critique is powerful, convincing and very timely, as the United Nations is starting to implement the agenda linked to the new 'sustainable development goals', it still remains only a partial account of the problems. In the following, I therefore briefly outline the background of the debate, and my reading of Easterly's position. Finally, I sketch the elements I believe to be missing from his account of the consequences of the West's failure to help the poorest people on the planet.

A background for the critique

While hopes for development aid remain high among many politicians and pundits in the Western world, the evidence is depressing. Surveying the literature on aid effectiveness, Doucouliagos and Paldam (2011), for example, show that foreign aid has on average had no discernible effect on long-run growth in developing countries. While a number of countries that received particularly large inflows of aid have dismal records, the most successful developing countries tend to be those that received little aid and by and large ignored advice from the World Bank, the United Nations and other international agencies.

Figure 2 provides three examples of neighbouring countries on very different development paths: Botswana, Zambia and Zimbabwe. Most pertinently, the figure clearly depicts the disastrous regime of Kenneth Kaunda, the undisputed ruler of Zambia from independence in 1964 until 1990. After declaring independence for the northern half of Rhodesia, Kaunda rapidly turned his new country into

Figure 2   **Development in Botswana, Zambia and Zimbabwe relative to the US**

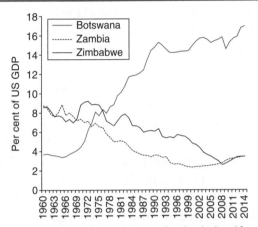

Note: data are a percentage of US real GDP per head, calculated from the Maddison Project: www.ggdc.net/maddison/maddison-project/home.htm.

a socialist one-party state and followed the international trend in development economics of state-led industrialisation. His policies were backed by aid donors who provided Zambia with foreign assistance amounting to roughly 10 per cent of GDP. Under his rule, Zambia nevertheless became poorer, both relative to the rest of the world and in absolute terms. By 1990, Zambian living standards had dropped approximately 20 per cent since independence. Yet, although Frederick Chiluba won the election in 1990 on promises of democracy and economic liberalisation, the long decline continued for another decade. As even more foreign aid flowed into a country ready for full-blown democracy, it allowed Chiluba to postpone or entirely abandon most of the promised reforms. It would take a further ten years and the example of the formerly communist countries in Europe before the Zambian government finally privatised the copper mines and started to liberalise other parts of the economy.

Zimbabwe historically formed the other part of the crown colonies of Rhodesia, and was known as Southern Rhodesia or simply Rhodesia until 1979. The country had unilaterally declared independence in 1965 and experienced rapid growth until the early 1970s. Zimbabwean GDP per head peaked in the mid 1970s at around the current level of Nigeria. Subsequently, the economy stagnated under the leadership of Robert Mugabe. As is evident from Figure 2, the situation briefly improved in the early 1990s, after which a series of disastrous policy choices dramatically worsened the situation. While aid inflows had initially decreased due to the ageing Mugabe's autocratic behaviour and evident disregard for the rule of law, flows increased again as a response to the social consequences of hyperinflation and a populist and failed land reform. The main change, according to AidData, was that the new aid flows were primarily directed to social purposes instead of more traditional economic development. Yet despite the substantial inflows of Western aid and attention, Zimbabwean living standards are now back to the level they were at in the late 1960s.

Zimbabwe's western neighbour, Botswana, took another route and has become what has been termed 'the secret tiger economy'. Living standards measured by real

GDP per head are now eleven times higher than at independence in 1966, life expectancy has increased by twelve years (despite the severe AIDS epidemic in the country), and Botswana has maintained a functioning democracy for all fifty years of independence. The quality of its institutions is also well ahead of that of Turkey and most of central and eastern Europe. In some ways, its development since the late 1960s has been more impressive than that of the better-known Asian tigers such as South Korea and Taiwan. Yet, since the mid 1990s, the country has received virtually no foreign aid but has continued to grow substantially faster than most other countries.

As these examples indicate, it is difficult if not impossible to talk about developing countries as one group with comparable problems or challenges and a similar set of solutions. Yet what is common to a majority of these countries is a history of large government failures with dire consequences, often actively supported by the World Bank, the United Nations or the hundreds of other Western donor organisations. Some voices still claim that foreign aid and other Western interventions work as intended. They continue to be influential in policy environments, but the dearth of positive examples has created 'aid fatigue' in developed countries since the 1990s.

In recent years, the work by Clemens et al. (2012) has nevertheless bolstered support for foreign aid by finding that 'early-impact aid' can affect the growth rate. Yet, with Easterly's particular critique in mind, it is ironic that Clemens et al. argue in favour of, for example, support for infrastructure and industrial development. The first attempts at replication of the Clemens approach indicate that the general findings may be spurious (Bjørnskov 2013; Roodman 2015). Despite the occasional study arguing that 'aid works', the academic consensus remains that the development effectiveness of foreign aid is close to zero.

In addition, many studies now document unintended consequences of aid and other Western interventions in the developing world. Independent thinkers such as Easterly, who can point to reasons why previous efforts have failed, are therefore sorely needed.

Easterly's main argument

Easterly's main argument consists of two basic observations. First, he notes that for as long as the West has provided so-called development assistance to poor or less developed countries, the causes of poverty and slow growth have been viewed as technical problems. And technical problems call for technical solutions. Development agencies from the British Colonial Office to the World Bank have therefore evolved into technocratic organisations. Second, Easterly notes that in order effectively to implement their grand schemes of technical development, these agencies have willingly colluded with some of the most autocratic governments in the world. His claim is that the combination of misdiagnosing development problems and trampling on poor people's basic rights has caused massive human suffering and prevented aid worth many billions of pounds from having any clearly positive effect.

Easterly starts by observing that 'there is something about technical solutions that is very, very seductive'. Technical solutions are quick fixes and their promise of delivering rapid development has lured many development economists, doctors and others within the development community to endorse autocratic methods. Most of them have undoubtedly privately favoured democracy, but have suffered from the illusion that dictatorships get things done. Part of the problem is, as Easterly has hinted several times, that at the heart of the development community is a deep bureaucratic distrust of poor people (Easterly 2002). The basic assumptions about poor people have changed very little since the days of Lord Hailey[1] and the belief persists that they are better off by being managed by experts from the development community. Easterly provides several highly entertaining, but also rather scary, examples of how technocratic proposals in recent UN and World Bank reports simply echo what Lord Hailey's expert report recommended about eighty years ago. Likewise, Hailey shared the same distrust in poor people's ability to govern themselves when he argued that 'Political liberties are meaningless unless they can be built up on a better foundation of social and economic progress' (cited in Wolton 2000: 108–9).

Easterly's main argument is that the problem 'is not a shortage of experts. It's a shortage of rights.' In his Hayek lecture and elsewhere, his main argument against 'experts'

---

1   Lord Hailey (1872–1969) was an administrator in British India, but also spent time in Africa, producing the 1938 African Survey, which proved influential in the movement for colonial reform.

is a combination of Hayekian concern with information problems and emphasis on the type of problems of political and bureaucratic accountability described by the literature on public choice and political economy. Easterly's argument is, in other words, firmly within the tradition of 'robust political economy' (Pennington 2011).

First, Easterly criticises the methods used by the World Bank and others to 'design' projects and programmes. This is a version of what Munger (2008: 512) calls Hayek's 'institutional design problem'. He summarises the problem as the standard situation where 'Government has no non-arbitrary means of acquiring, or even estimating, the information required to solve the problem that markets have failed to solve.' In the context of development initiatives, donor organisations (such as the World Bank, USAID or SIDA) start by perceiving a situation of immense market failures and past political failures that caused countries in Africa and Asia to be poor. As Easterly convincingly shows, they then go on to formulate these perceived problems as technical challenges and then devise some sort of technical solution: delivering mosquito nets, draining swamps or moving entire populations to provide room for a new dam.

Yet, many – perhaps most – of these projects eventually fail because the organisations have not understood the original problems and the actual context. In other words, donor organisations ignore local knowledge to an alarming extent, and fail to realise the value of dispersed, localised and sometimes intangible knowledge and skills at the local level. Easterly therefore echoes Hayek (1945: 521), who warned against technical solutions by stressing that the 'problem of society is thus not merely a problem of how to allocate "given" resources'. The main problem is that the donor organisations have little information on the actual problems of poor people and literally no way of knowing which kinds of initiatives are likely to work and which will fail.

Another part of Hayek and Easterly's outline of the problem is that donors do not operate in 'virgin' institutional territory. As Hayek (1945) argued, the information needed to enable governments to design proper regulations does not exist without the market. It is, in other words, impossible to know what poor people might achieve on their own without the distorting presence of donors and autocratic government. In many ways, the past actions of donors have willingly destroyed any information that might have led them to question the impact of their interventions. Their own activity and the interventions and policies of regimes they have tacitly or explicitly supported have erased that information. Yet they still act as if their knowledge is not only complete, but also superior to the information that is held at the local level. In the context of government interventions in rich countries, Hayek would later go on to call this assumption a 'fatal conceit'. Easterly demonstrates that it is no less fatal in developing countries.

The second element of Easterly's powerful critique has already been touched upon: the willing collusion with undemocratic, and often strongly authoritarian, regimes. In his lecture, Easterly, for example, outlines the policy of the World Bank simply to ignore any mention of democracy or political rights in order not to offend any recipient governments. He also provides numerous examples in both the lecture and his other writings of how autocratic regimes with no respect for human rights make the implementation of technical solutions much easier. Poor people, their activities and their basic rights are merely in the way of grandiose projects that economists in Washington, political scientists in Paris or anthropologists in Stockholm 'know' is best for them. However, without those rights, local initiative vanishes, political elites and markets fail. To some extent, Easterly here echoes Hernando de Soto (2000) and his emphasis on effective property rights as a basis for sustainable long-run development. Without enforceable title to their land, the incentives to invest in it and the possibility of using it as collateral, disappear – leaving poor people with few options to improve their lot.

While Easterly does not deny that some projects and programmes occasionally do good, his main argument may be that something like a Hippocratic Oath should govern all development work: first and foremost, the development community ought to get out of the way of poor people in order not to do harm.

What is missing in Easterly's argument?

However, while Easterly's two-pronged critique of the current foreign aid regime from a Hayekian information angle and from a rights-based point of view is as insightful as it is challenging to current practice, he almost leaves out an entire line of attack: inflows of foreign aid, very much like the discovery of certain natural resources, have negative unintended consequences. This is arguably the main weakness in an otherwise very convincing set of arguments, because what is left out is an account of what Paul Mosley once dubbed the 'micro–macro paradox'.

The micro–macro paradox is a description of the seemingly impossible situation where foreign aid interventions can be shown on average to have a positive effect on development when measured at the household, local or regional level, but no effect when estimated at the national level. Ignoring the paradox means that if one has to account for the fact that foreign aid does not affect long-run development, any reading of Easterly's critique must necessarily imply that projects, programmes and other aid interventions on average have zero effect. In other words, the consequences of information problems and rights violations must be so severe that the economic or social footprint of any reasonably successful project is erased by those of equally disastrous projects. I am not sure that I am willing to go that far in criticising development work on the ground. Neither, do I believe, is Easterly himself.

Instead, a long line of studies since the late 1990s have documented that foreign aid – and other international interventions – has serious side effects. In the Question and Answer (Q&A) session after the lecture, Easterly himself referred to these studies. He noted the recent claim by last year's recipient of the Nobel Prize in economics, Angus Deaton, that aid to dictators 'arguably makes them likely to last longer, that they have more money from outside support, and can ignore domestic factors because they have more outside money supporting them'. Indeed, Amanda

Licht (2010) has documented how aid helps dictatorial regimes to survive for longer, but has no such effect when the incumbent government is reasonably democratic. To some extent, this may even be a situation that donor organisations welcome. Yet the problems do not end here.

One of the best known side-effects of foreign aid is Dutch Disease: the situation where the exchange and spending effects of inflows of aid cause a real exchange rate appreciation. The consequence is a loss of international competitiveness and a shrinking manufacturing and export sector (Rajan and Subramanian 2011). Similar Dutch Disease effects are well documented in the context of oil and gas exports and are considered a main element of what is known as 'the natural resource curse' – that resource-rich countries remain among the world's poorest. In both cases, the effect of inflows of aid or resource revenue results in a contraction of either the modern sectors of the economy or sectors in which the country used to have a comparative advantage. This effect may be even more pernicious in the poorest developing countries, where the comparative advantage that is harmed is in agriculture, where a large and very poor majority of the population works.

As Easterly hinted at in the Q&A session, Western aid also tends to distort the political incentives in recipient countries. Stephen Knack, one of Easterly's former colleagues at the World Bank, has in several studies documented how aid causes politicians to postpone or cancel reforms of the judicial system as well as democratising reforms (Bräutigam and Knack 2004; Heckelman and Knack 2008). Deaton (2013) has also spoken out against this side effect and stressed how aid flows make political elites fiscally independent of the rest of the population. This problem, which was originally described by Peter Bauer (1975), implies that unelected regimes in particular need only be accountable to the donor community and not their own populations. In return, as Easterly documents, donors are more than willing to help these regimes implement grand plans regardless of the human rights of their citizens. When such purposes become salient, the type of strong and politically independent judiciaries that were central to European development merely become a nuisance. Inflows of aid and natural resource rents thus allow the regimes to prevent the development of growth-enhancing institutions.

A part of the tragedy of Western interventions and help in the last half century is therefore not merely the collusion between donors and authoritarian regimes, but also the unintended consequence of holding back democracy and good institutions. However, once very poor countries democratise, it is clear that their citizens start demanding what the West has: good and transparent institutions, respect for basic rights and economic progress. Democratisation itself therefore often brings about a change for the better, although this change may not be in the interests of small entrenched elites.

For example, the 20 African countries that today have sufficiently democratic institutions to allow peaceful changes of government have substantially better and more politically independent judiciaries than the 34 countries with no democracy. The only African country to remain thoroughly democratic since independence – Botswana – also remains a powerful example of the consequences of taking political and human rights seriously under even the poorest conditions. In addition, Botswana has resisted the temptation to implement populist redistributive and fiscal policy that aid inflows could also fund. In most other developing countries the negative incentive effects of receiving aid appear to imply everything from refraining from servicing international debt obligations to outright fraud (Bjørnskov and Schröder 2013; Werker et al. 2009).

Assessing the consequences of foreign aid or other interventions in poor countries is not simply a matter of evaluating separate projects, programmes or initiatives, and, at the macro level, estimates of their effectiveness have been consistently disappointing. The response of the international community has been a mixture of denial and systematic mission creep. As Easterly (2009) himself has shown, the list of intended consequences has expanded as the assessments of the previously intended consequences turned out to be disappointing. What to assess has therefore become a moving target, while the side effects persist.

Which way next?

The point of this chapter is not that Easterly is wrong, but that the picture he paints of how foreign aid and other Western interventions work and how they have failed is incomplete. The knowledge of what these interventions have done is itself far from complete, and some questions remain highly disputed. Yet, it seems safe to say that the problem is not just the projects or the way they are implemented. A fuller account must, as Easterly hinted in the Hayek lecture, include the way in which aid distorts incentives in the political system and effectively rewards autocratic and irresponsible behaviour. In a perhaps paradoxical way, the view of development work taken by the world's pre-eminent critical voice may be too optimistic.

The question one must ask oneself – and that most sceptical development economists ask in public – is whether all these efforts are in vain: is the conclusion that nothing works and therefore nothing can be done? The answer is no, although the problems documented by Easterly and others must necessarily leave a much reduced role for Western aid and interventions. First, some types of project seem to perform relatively well. Deaton (2013), for example, emphasises aid for public health purposes, where the investment of relatively limited resources has made a clear difference fighting malaria, HIV/AIDS and specific tropical diseases. These types tend not to be 'fungible', i.e. do not allow governments to reduce their own spending on the goal and thus implicitly redirect Western funds to other goals.

In the study of overall aid effectiveness, the question that occupies minds today is whether it is instead possible to either find specific types of aid that work as intended or identify specific conditions under which aid works. Dreher et al. (2016) indicate that aid given for strategic, political purposes is less effective, while at least some aid given without particular political aims in mind may work. My own research suggests that reconstruction aid following wars or natural disasters can be effective (Bjørnskov 2013). Which particular types of aid work under which specific conditions nevertheless remains an open question.

However, research at both the micro level and the macro level points in a particular – and particularly unpopular – direction. It implies that most interventions have made no difference, some have had adverse effects and the unintended consequences are mostly negative. When taking Easterly and other sceptics seriously, it implies that fewer resources and fewer aid workers are needed. Easterly's main message is that we need to be much more humble, and start listening to the knowledge and insights of poor people in developing countries.

References

Bauer, P. T. (1972) *Dissent on Development*. Cambridge, MA: Harvard University Press.

Bjørnskov, C. (2013) Types of foreign aid. Department of Economics and Business, Working Paper 2013-08, Aarhus University.

Bjørnskov, C. and Schröder, P. (2013) Are debt repayment incentives undermined by foreign aid? *Journal of Comparative Economics* 41: 1073–91.

Bräutigam, D. A. and Knack, S. (2004) Foreign aid, institutions, and governance in Sub-Saharan Africa. *Economic Development and Cultural Change* 52: 256–85.

Clemens, M. A., Radelet, S., Bhavnani, R. R. and Bazzi, S. (2012) Counting chickens when they hatch: timing and the effects of aid on growth. *Economic Journal* 122: 590–617.

Deaton, A. (2013) *The Great Escape: Health, Wealth, and the Origins of Inequality.* Princeton University Press.

De Soto, H. (2000) *The Mystery of Capital: Why Capitalism Triumphs in the West and Fails Everywhere Else.* New York: Basic Books.

Doucouliagos, H. and Paldam, M. (2011) The ineffectiveness of development aid on growth: an update. *European Journal of Political Economy* 27: 399–404.

Dreher, A., Eichenauer, V. and Gehring, K. (2016) Geopolitics, aid and growth: the impact of UN Security Council membership on the effectiveness of aid. *World Bank Economic Review.* http://doi.org/bnh8.

Easterly, W. (2002) The cartel of good intentions: the problem of bureaucracy in foreign aid. *Journal of Policy Reform* 5: 223–50.

Easterly, W. (2009) Can the West save Africa? *Journal of Economic Literature* 47: 373–44.

Hayek, F. A. (1945) The use of knowledge in society. *American Economic Review* 35: 519–30.

Heckelman, J. and Knack, S. (2008) Foreign aid and market-liberalizing reform. *Economica* 75: 524–48.

Licht, A. A. (2010) Coming into money: the impact of foreign aid on leader survival. *Journal of Conflict Resolution* 54: 58–87.

Munger, M. C. (2008) Economic choice, political decision, and the problem of limits. *Public Choice* 137: 507–22.

Pennington, M. (2011) *Robust Political Economy: Classical Liberalism and the Future of Public Policy.* Cheltenham: Edward Elgar.

Rajan, R. G. and Subramanian, A. (2011) Aid, Dutch disease, and manufacturing growth. *Journal of Development Economics* 94: 106–18.

Roodman, D. M. (2015) A replication of 'Counting chickens when they hatch' (*Economic Journal* 2012). *Public Finance Review* 43(2): 256–81.

Werker, E. D., Ahmed, F. Z. and Cohen, C. (2009) How is foreign aid spent? Evidence from a natural experiment. *American Economic Journal: Macroeconomics* 1: 225–44.

Wolton, S. (2000) *Lord Hailey, the Colonial Office and the Politics of Race and Empire in the Second World War: The Loss of White Prestige.* Oxford: Palgrave Macmillan.

5 ENTREPRENEURSHIP, SOCIAL ENGAGEMENT AND AFRICAN DEVELOPMENT IN THE TWENTY-FIRST CENTURY

A commentary on William Easterly's lecture

Sylvie Aboa-Bradwell

Introduction

There is a longstanding tradition of criticism of foreign aid and charity as means of development for poor countries. In the 1960s, Peter Bauer deduced that 'indefinite aid – what might be termed mainstream foreign aid – has not served to bring about an appreciable rise in living standards in under-developed countries' (Bauer 1966: 44). At present, one of the most prominent exponents of this tradition is William Easterly. In his Hayek lecture he denounces the tendency of foreign aid and development practitioners to prioritise technocratic solutions to poverty over poor people's rights. In the case of Africa, he points out that, despite colluding with autocrats since colonial times to perpetrate human rights abuses against African populations while purportedly seeking their prosperity, Western technocrats have failed to trigger development in this continent.

It is particularly appropriate to highlight the direct link between current African underdevelopment, human rights abuses and Africa's colonial past.[1] The colonisation of the northern part of Africa by Arabs, which started with the Muslim expansion in the seventh century, entrenched a socio-economic infrastructure based on the exploitation and enslavement of weaker groups deemed unbelievers or uncivilised. Instead of developing their nations, the beneficiaries of this exploitative system, both Arabs and Africans, strove to invade other territories to procure more slaves and more people to exploit.[2] Western involvement through the transatlantic slave trade first, and colonisation later, strengthened this exploitative system and expanded it all over Africa.

In African societies traditionally geared towards communitarianism and solidarity, the many centuries of colonisation, slave trade and enslavement of subjugated populations gave rise to ruling and entrepreneurial elites that were selfish, rapacious and uncaring.[3] The decolonisation

---

1   Contrary to the impression conveyed by some scholars and activists, colonisation is an age-old practice in which most human groups have engaged, and not simply the preserve of white Westerners. Cases in point include not only the Arab colonisation mentioned here, but also the colonial expansion in central and southern Africa of Bantu groups such as the Zulus, Betis, etc.

2   The Kanem–Bornu Empire, which existed from the ninth century till 1900, and which at its peak covered territories in modern-day Nigeria, Chad, Cameroon, Niger and Libya, provides an illustration of how, for over a thousand years, the economic system of vast swathes of Africa was based on colonial expansion, slavery and exploitation.

3   Rather than depending on good governance for legitimacy, rulers could often rely on brute force, dictatorship and colonial allies to secure and maintain power. Equally, entrepreneurs did not need to satisfy local customers and develop their communities to enrich themselves; they could do so by simply selling, exploiting and abusing unprotected populations.

of the African continent in the twentieth century did not change this state of affairs. As John Mukum Mbaku asserts, in postcolonial Africa 'constitution making was top-down, elite-driven, opportunistic and reluctant' because of the dictatorial nature of most governments. This encouraged entrepreneurs 'to invest in rent seeking, corruption and other forms of opportunism' (Mbaku 2007: 4).

There is thus a fundamental difference between the context of Western countries, such as the UK, during their developing stage in the nineteenth century, and that of most African states now. The defining characteristics of the former included the rule of law, accountability of leaders, as well as independence of the judiciary, press and other institutions necessary for sustainable development, peace and justice. Conversely, what currently prevails in the overwhelming majority of African countries is not justice or the rule of law, but the arbitrary will of unaccountable autocrats and their corrupt cronies, including opulent entrepreneurs.

This contrast explains why, whereas the philanthropic endeavours of wealthy business people, such as the Quakers George Cadbury and Joseph Rowntree, proved to be catalysts for positive social change and prosperity in the UK, foreign handouts and philanthropy have failed to trigger development in Africa for decades. In the African context described above, philanthropy, charity and foreign aid became, and remain, additional agents of the pauperisation, oppression and exploitation of African people. Avaricious African rulers collude with self-interested local entrepreneurs, foreign governments, multinationals and charities, to steal and squander their countries' wealth and natural resources, while relying on foreign handouts to sustain their citizens.[4]

Nevertheless, it would be erroneous to assume that the commercial sector and business people cannot spearhead movements capable of triggering the structural, economic and social transformation Africa urgently needs. There is a glimmer of hope for the continent, thanks to the recent emergence of socially conscious African entrepreneurs and activists.[5] They are reluctant to embrace the traditional charity model of engagement with Africa, which views and treats Africans as helpless victims in perpetual need of handouts. Instead, they leverage their entrepreneurial skills, innovative ideas and strategies, time and resources to set up businesses, social enterprises, leadership training companies and think tanks with enormous potential as catalysts for positive change. To exemplify this positive trend, this chapter analyses the background, vision, challenges and achievements of three organisations: Acosphere, the Policy Centre for African Peoples and GoGetters.

---

4 For an illustration of this state of affairs, see, for instance, Anderson (2014).

5 The word 'African' is used here to refer to Africans living both in the continent and in the diaspora. As the only continent that has been deprived of millions of people by centuries of slave trade, Africa should, and has historically been eager to, capitalise on the input from diaspora members. Furthermore, just as the impetus for the decolonisation of the African continent in the twentieth century started in the diaspora, the diaspora could also spearhead its positive socio-economic transformation in the twenty-first century.

Background and vision

These three organisations vary in nature, modus operandi and objectives. They do, however, share some common features. They are new, relatively small, innovative and forward-looking. Above all, they are very ambitious in terms of their vision for the socio-economic improvement of African populations, as they reflect their founders' conviction that it is incumbent on them to bring about development and positive social transformation in Africa and among the African diaspora.

After many years working in the corporate sector, Gilles Acogny and Nadia Mensah Acogny, from Senegal and Benin respectively, felt the need to make a difference in companies by changing beliefs and behavioural patterns. Thus, in 2005, they founded Acosphere, a business that specialises in management consultancy, operational services and transformational training. The key purpose of Acosphere is to instil in companies the twin beliefs that happiness in the workplace can generate high performance and income, and that such outcomes can be achieved by focusing on people and their talents. Its activities, which started in Europe, have progressively expanded into different parts of the world following requests from clients, including multinationals such as Xerox, Barclays, BNP Paribas, Ecobank, Aggreko and Orange.

In the last three years, Gilles Acogny and Nadia Mensah Acogny have chosen to intensify their strategic focus on the African continent. Their vision is to channel all the knowledge, experience, results and success they have accumulated into the workforce of African companies. They are convinced that 'Africa *is* the next frontier' and thus 'definitely the place to be in this period and age.' Furthermore, as Africans, they feel that the time has come 'to give back, both from a business and personal standpoint'.[6]

In 2008 I, a Cameroonian national, created the Policy Centre for African Peoples (PCAP). As an entrepreneur, writer and educator, I have resolved to end the monopolisation of discussions on African topics 'by non-governmental organisations, celebrities, politicians and entrepreneurs purporting to seek the development of Africa when in fact, their modus operandi and, in some cases, their existence, depended on the perpetuation of age-old myths that were hindering this development' (Aboa-Bradwell 2014). Thus, I founded PCAP to provide a platform for the engagement and education of African individuals and important stakeholders in Africa, the UK, Europe and elsewhere.

To realise this vision, PCAP operates as an independent think tank. It carries out research, organises debates and public campaigns and hosts events on topics that are crucial to Africans and relevant partners. PCAP has established itself as an organisation capable of leading discussions and influencing policies on subjects such as African development, education, human rights, social justice and democracy. A distinctive feature of PCAP – and the key to its success – is its strategic, political and financial independence. It is the only UK-based think tank led and

---

6   Author's interview with Gilles Acogny and Nadia Mensah Acogny on 13 April 2016.

financially controlled by Africans. As Professor Easterly has asserted elsewhere, 'In any human endeavour, the people paying the bills are the ones to keep happy. The big problem with foreign aid and other Western efforts to transform the Rest is that the people paying the bills are rich people who have very little knowledge of poor people' (Easterly 2006: 15). By eschewing the traditional model of African organisations funded and supervised by international donors and institutions, PCAP has ensured that all the policies it advocates are independent, informed by the aspirations, realities and experiences of African people, and primarily aimed at benefiting African countries and populations.

The third organisation, GoGetters (GG), was founded in the UK in 2013 by five young Africans led by Sierra Leone–born Alieu Fofana. A business and management graduate and a qualified chartered accountant, Fofana, the CEO of GG, also works in PricewaterhouseCoopers' Africa Business Group. He and his fellow GG founders were, and remain, convinced that the solution to most of Africa's problems, including the development conundrum, is to harness and unleash the potential of its greatest asset: its people.

The vision of GG is to release African people's potential 'by fostering collaboration, and by eradicating the habits and behaviours that are holding the continent back'.[7] To achieve this, GG operates as a network of African entrepreneurs and Africa-oriented investors that provides its members with the tools, space and structure they need to build

---

7 Interview with Alieu Fofana on 12 February 2016.

trust, inspire and support one another. It also organises educational and motivational workshops for entrepreneurs, professionals, youths and communities both in Africa and in the diaspora. The GG executive team, which includes five members in the UK and four in Africa, is committed to the realisation of what it calls the 'African Promise'. This concept expresses the desire of GG to ingrain in Africans, and other people wanting to do business or live happily in Africa, the idea that they must take action to trigger the positive change that this continent needs to fulfil its promise; that is, to become the land of opportunities and prosperity that its outstanding beauty and its human, natural, cultural and other resources should enable it to be.[8]

Challenges

Many hurdles hamper the fulfilment of the respective visions of Acosphere, the Policy Centre for African Peoples and GoGetters. Some of these relate to the costs of doing business in the African continent, especially for Acosphere.

The main obstacle for PCAP and GG is the corrupt environment in which they are operating or seek to operate. For instance, Kenya is, alongside Nigeria, South Africa, Sierra Leone, Ghana, Rwanda and Sudan, one of the many African states where both organisations either have worked or have key stakeholders. Willy Mutunga, Kenya's Chief Justice, recently lamented that his country has been

---

8 For further exploration of the African Promise concept, see Fofana (2015a,b) and James-Odukoya (2015).

transformed into a 'bandit economy' controlled by corrupt business people and politicians ready to kill or exile those opposing their cartels, and added that the situation was not much better in Nigeria, Africa's largest economy (Lindijer 2016).

Under such circumstances, the executives of GG are understandably reluctant to have their specific experiences with corruption in Kenya, Nigeria and other African nations detailed here. Nevertheless, they admit that they have been confronted with bribery demands. As a think tank committed to the advancement of socio-political reforms in the African continent, PCAP has forcefully campaigned against and publicly denounced corruption and misappropriation of funds by African leaders and their cronies. For instance, in an article recently published on AllAfrica.com (the most popular news and comment site throughout Africa) PCAP stated that the leaders of African countries threatened by Islamic insurgents 'must realise that good governance is the most effective weapon they urgently need to acquire to overcome this threat. For too long, they have siphoned off, mismanaged and squandered their nations' resources while relying on foreign donors to provide basic services to their people. This has to stop' (Aboa-Bradwell 2015).

The sad truth, though, is that such malpractices will not end any time soon. Many African countries are, and for the foreseeable future will remain, societies where opportunities are restricted to a clique of self-serving individuals determined to pursue and preserve their interests. Consequently, the governmental, private or social infrastructure that could facilitate the achievement of the goals of new and progressive organisations like PCAP and GG is generally lacking. Furthermore, there is an acute dearth of avenues for such entities to secure strategic partnerships with established African magnates who could act as their backers and mentors. Although many wealthy African business people have created charities and foundations, these are, more often than not, focused on implementing projects aimed at fulfilling the basic needs of the most deprived. Such activities, however helpful, cannot generate enough jobs for the millions of unemployed African youths, or kick-start the socio-economic transformation and development that Africa requires.[9]

Achievements

Despite these challenges, GoGetters, the Policy Centre for African Peoples and Acosphere have accumulated many outstanding achievements.

In its ten years of existence, Acosphere has managed to serve and satisfy a wide variety of clients, including, most recently, large African companies wanting to upgrade the skills of their teams.

The achievements of GG include: filming three documentaries; organising several entrepreneurial workshops

---

9 A view also expressed by Thierry Zomahoun, President and CEO of the Next Einstein Forum, a platform created in 2013 to bring together leading thinkers in science, policy, industry and civil society in Africa in order to leverage science to solve global challenges. 'No nation has ever achieved development by just focusing on basic needs,' Zomahoun said in a recent TV interview, Al Jazeera, 10 March 2016.

in Africa; launching the Start-Up West Africa website (http://startupwestafrica.org/) and writing and publishing the Start-Up West Africa Report. The impetus for shooting the documentaries was GG's desire to explore the entrepreneurial environment, particularly the technology start-up ecosystem, of six sub-Saharan African countries, namely South Africa, Kenya, Rwanda, Ghana, Nigeria and Sierra Leone. Their tour of the aforementioned African nations lasted from September 2013 to March 2014.[10] The Start-Up West Africa website provides thousands of people across the globe with free and easy access to data, including West African technology start-ups, job search, events and investors. A bottom-up approach is the cornerstone of the success of this service, as the content is primarily crowdsourced, and the data updated on a daily basis. In 2015, GG began publishing the Start-Up West Africa Report. The first report focuses on Nigeria, and provides people interested in investing there with analysis and data including market size, key players, regulations, challenges, opportunities and local culture (for further details, see Akinnaike 2016).

The Policy Centre for African Peoples has achieved much since its creation in 2008. For instance, to maximise its capacity to engage and educate African individuals and key stakeholders on African and other topics that are of relevance to them, the think tank launched the PCAP Policy Brief in January 2011. The first issue, 'An Unsung African

---

10 The documentaries, findings, workshops and other activities related to the GG team's tour are detailed on their website; GoGetters, 'Our Journey' http://go-getters.co.uk/our-journey/ (accessed 20 April 2016).

Marvel', discussing Somaliland's achievement of democracy and peace, and the need for its recognition, was included in a book commemorating the twentieth anniversary of Somaliland's declaration of independence. The latest PCAP Policy Brief, 'The Battle for Africa's Soul in the 21st Century', an in-depth discussion of the topics of democracy, development and peace in the African continent, was recently selected for inclusion in a book on Africa in the twenty-first century, to be published in late 2016.

One of PCAP's main goals is the promotion of a new and positive narrative about Africa, in order to replace non-Africans' age-old use of foreign aid and charity as tools for engaging with Africa with more progressive and effective policies. PCAP has undertaken a wide range of activities to achieve this. For instance, the think tank partnered with the filmmaker Colin Izod and the broadcaster Henry Bonsu to produce a documentary entitled *Pitching Africa*, which followed PCAP as it gave a platform to Africans and African diaspora members with outstanding business proposals and ideas on the development of Africa and African communities.

In addition to the launch of the documentary in 2011, PCAP has hosted several conferences to brief potential investors about business opportunities in Africa. These included *Pitching Africa in the City* in 2013.

Lessons and recommendations

The drive and determination of the founders and teams of the Policy Centre for African Peoples, GoGetters and

Acosphere give them enormous potential as catalysts for the positive transformation of Africa in the entrepreneurial, economic, political and social spheres.

In order to achieve their full potential, PCAP and GG need to do the following: monetise their experiences, expertise and contacts; establish strategic and mutually beneficial partnerships with like-minded individuals and organisations; and strive harder to contribute towards a new narrative about Africa and a change in the manner in which relevant people and institutions engage with this continent. For instance, rather than merely enabling the identification and location of the stakeholders listed on the Start-Up West Africa website, the GG executives could consider becoming marketing and development partners of the most promising African start-ups that need more resources to either expand or strengthen their work. The additional funds and profits generated would not only lead to the expansion and consolidation of the start-ups, but also give GG the opportunity to obtain the money necessary to finance its projects. PCAP, for its part, could capitalise on the success of the *Pitching Africa* series. It could host Dragons' Den–style sessions that would provide a platform for aspiring entrepreneurs from Africa and the diaspora to find investors.

Zambian-born economist Dambisa Moyo (2009: xix) famously asserted: 'The notion that aid can alleviate systematic poverty, and has done so, is a myth. Millions in Africa are poorer today because of aid; misery and poverty have not ended but have increased.' Despite the fame and soundness of Moyo's critique of foreign aid to

Africa, the narrative and initiatives about this continent are still overwhelmingly dominated by the philanthropists and governments that prioritise engaging with Africans on the basis of charity, as William Easterly's lecture demonstrates.

Together, organisations such as those I have described should promote a new narrative about Africa that eschews charity and foreign aid and, instead, prioritises the leverage of African ideas, resources and skills including entrepreneurial expertise, leadership training, advocacy and social engagement as catalysts for development and positive transformation in Africa.

This could result in concrete projects that would break the age-old vicious circle of mistreatment of African populations and the squandering of national resources by unaccountable African elites and their foreign partners, dependency on handouts from wealthy donors and chronic mass poverty. In addition, the combination of such initiatives and a new African-inspired narrative about the continent could create a powerful firewall against the radical Islamic ideology and terrorist attacks that are currently threatening the stability of not only Nigeria, Africa's biggest economy and most populous nation, but also many other African countries.

Conclusion

Reflecting on the 40-year anniversary of the African Development Bank (AfDB), an institution created in 1964 to promote economic development and social advancement in Africa, Sir Lawrence Ukwu (2004: 1) lamented that AfDB had utterly failed to fulfil its mission, since 'the average African is worse off' and poverty 'is ravaging the continent'. An even more contrite admission of failure should be expressed by the proponents of charity and foreign aid as means of development for Africa. They have spent many more decades depriving its people of agency, backing unaccountable tyrants and human rights abuses in this continent and using Africans as laboratory rats for all sorts of failed and damaging experiments. Easterly's Hayek lecture makes this very clear.

Unlike many Western countries that systematised and professionalised the charitable engagement model after establishing the rule of law, mutual respect and commitment to common national goals, the overwhelming majority of African states had a centuries-old tradition of abuse and exploitation of their populations by local elites and their foreign partners. Thus, charity and foreign aid have not, and cannot, act as catalysts for development in Africa. They have been, and seem bound to remain, vectors of pervasive injustice, corruption and squandering of national resources as well as inhumane treatment and disenfranchisement of citizens by unaccountable leaders and their cronies.

Better alternatives to charity and foreign aid include socially conscious African entrepreneurs, thinkers and activists using their financial resources, skills and innovative ideas to promote economic development, foster education and combat the negative habits and mindsets that are hampering Africa's progress.

Easterly is right. The future does not lie in foreign aid, outside experts or military intervention. Fortunately, a growing number of organisations are articulating the case for rights in Africa and, like PCAP, GG and Acosphere, in different ways, can empower Africans to control their own development from the grass roots up.

References

Aboa-Bradwell, S. (2014) Myth-busting: a *sine qua non* for Africa's 21st century development. Global Development Goals 2014-UNA UK, October. Available at www.policycap.org/wp-advocacy/uploads/2014/12/United-Nations-A-UK-Article-by-Sylvie-Aboa-Bradwell.pdf (accessed 15 April 2016).

Aboa-Bradwell, S. (2015) Je suis Africa. AllAfrica.com, 28 January. Available at http://allafrica.com/stories/201501281527.html (accessed 18 August 2016).

Akinnaike, S. (2015) Start-Up West Africa Report: Nigeria Edition, 25 May. Available at http://startupwestafrica.org/blog/ (accessed 19 March 2016).

Anderson, M. (2014) Aid to Africa: donations from West mask '$60bn looting' of continent. *The Guardian*, 15 July. Available at www.theguardian.com/global-development/2014/jul/15/aid-africa-west-looting-continent (accessed 26 February 2016).

Bauer, P. T. (1966) Foreign aid: an instrument for progress? In *Two Views on Aid to Developing Countries* (ed. P. T. Bauer and B. Ward). London: Institute of Economic Affairs.

Easterly, W. (2006) *The White Man's Burden: Why the West's Efforts to Aid the Rest Have Done so Much Ill and so Little Good.* Oxford University Press.

Fofana, A. (2015a) The African Promise Part 1, GoGetters Blog, 6 May. Available at http://go-getters.co.uk/the-african-prom ise-part-1/ (accessed 17 March 2016).

Fofana, A. (2015b) The African Promise Part 3: Interview with Paul Cleal, PwC Managing Partner of the UK/Africa Alliance. GG Blog, 16 June. Available at http://go-getters.co.uk/the-african -promise-part-3/ (accessed 17 March 2016).

James-Odukoya, T. (2015) The African Promise Part 2. GG Blog, 18 May. Available at http://go-getters.co.uk/the-african-pro mise-part-2-2/ (accessed 17 March 2016).

Lindijer, K. (2016) Kenya has become a 'bandit economy', says Chief Justice Willy Mutunga. *African Arguments*, 11 January. Available at http://africanarguments.org/2016/01/11/kenya -has-become-a-bandit-economy-says-chief-justice-willy-mu tunga/ (accessed 8 March 2016).

Mbaku, J. M. (2007) *Corruption in Africa: Causes, Consequences and Cleanups.* Lanham: Lexington Books.

Moyo, D. (2009) *Dead Aid: Why Aid Is Not Working and How There Is Another Way for Africa.* London: Allen Lane.

Ukwu, L. (2004) *Realities of ADB Operations and Future Challenges: Insider Knowledge of Ten Years Coverage of the Bank* Lagos: Benneen & Tokel.

ABOUT THE IEA

The Institute is a research and educational charity (No. CC 235 351), limited by guarantee. Its mission is to improve understanding of the fundamental institutions of a free society by analysing and expounding the role of markets in solving economic and social problems.

The IEA achieves its mission by:

- a high-quality publishing programme
- conferences, seminars, lectures and other events
- outreach to school and college students
- brokering media introductions and appearances

The IEA, which was established in 1955 by the late Sir Antony Fisher, is an educational charity, not a political organisation. It is independent of any political party or group and does not carry on activities intended to affect support for any political party or candidate in any election or referendum, or at any other time. It is financed by sales of publications, conference fees and voluntary donations.

In addition to its main series of publications the IEA also publishes a quarterly journal, *Economic Affairs*.

The IEA is aided in its work by a distinguished international Academic Advisory Council and an eminent panel of Honorary Fellows. Together with other academics, they review prospective IEA publications, their comments being passed on anonymously to authors. All IEA papers are therefore subject to the same rigorous independent refereeing process as used by leading academic journals.

IEA publications enjoy widespread classroom use and course adoptions in schools and universities. They are also sold throughout the world and often translated/reprinted.

Since 1974 the IEA has helped to create a worldwide network of 100 similar institutions in over 70 countries. They are all independent but share the IEA's mission.

Views expressed in the IEA's publications are those of the authors, not those of the Institute (which has no corporate view), its Managing Trustees, Academic Advisory Council members or senior staff.

Members of the Institute's Academic Advisory Council, Honorary Fellows, Trustees and Staff are listed on the following page.

The Institute gratefully acknowledges financial support for its publications programme and other work from a generous benefaction by the late Professor Ronald Coase.

Other books recently published by the IEA include:

Which Road Ahead – Government or Market?
Oliver Knipping & Richard Wellings
Hobart Paper 171; ISBN 978-0-255-36619-9; £10.00

The Future of the Commons – Beyond Market Failure and Government Regulation
Elinor Ostrom et al.
Occasional Paper 148; ISBN 978-0-255-36653-3; £10.00

Redefining the Poverty Debate – Why a War on Markets Is No Substitute for a War on Poverty
Kristian Niemietz
Research Monograph 67; ISBN 978-0-255-36652-6; £12.50

The Euro – the Beginning, the Middle … and the End?
Edited by Philip Booth
Hobart Paperback 39; ISBN 978-0-255-36680-9; £12.50

The Shadow Economy
Friedrich Schneider & Colin C. Williams
Hobart Paper 172; ISBN 978-0-255-36674-8; £12.50

Quack Policy – Abusing Science in the Cause of Paternalism
Jamie Whyte
Hobart Paper 173; ISBN 978-0-255-36673-1; £10.00

Foundations of a Free Society
Eamonn Butler
Occasional Paper 149; ISBN 978-0-255-36687-8; £12.50

The Government Debt Iceberg
Jagadeesh Gokhale
Research Monograph 68; ISBN 978-0-255-36666-3; £10.00
A U-Turn on the Road to Serfdom
Grover Norquist
Occasional Paper 150; ISBN 978-0-255-36686-1; £10.00

New Private Monies – A Bit-Part Player?
Kevin Dowd
Hobart Paper 174; ISBN 978-0-255-36694-6; £10.00

From Crisis to Confidence – Macroeconomics after the Crash
Roger Koppl
Hobart Paper 175; ISBN 978-0-255-36693-9; £12.50

Advertising in a Free Society
Ralph Harris and Arthur Seldon
With an introduction by Christopher Snowdon
Hobart Paper 176; ISBN 978-0-255-36696-0; £12.50

Other IEA publications

Comprehensive information on other publications and the wider work of the IEA can be found at www.iea.org.uk. To order any publication please see below.

Personal customers

Orders from personal customers should be directed to the IEA:

Clare Rusbridge
IEA
2 Lord North Street
FREEPOST LON10168
London SW1P 3YZ
Tel: 020 7799 8907. Fax: 020 7799 2137
Email: sales@iea.org.uk

Trade customers

All orders from the book trade should be directed to the IEA's distributor:

NBN International (IEA Orders)
Orders Dept.
NBN International
10 Thornbury Road
Plymouth PL6 7PP
Tel: 01752 202301, Fax: 01752 202333
Email: orders@nbninternational.com

IEA subscriptions

The IEA also offers a subscription service to its publications. For a single annual payment (currently £42.00 in the UK), subscribers receive every monograph the IEA publishes. For more information please contact:

Clare Rusbridge
Subscriptions
IEA
2 Lord North Street
FREEPOST LON10168
London SW1P 3YZ
Tel: 020 7799 8907, Fax: 020 7799 2137
Email: crusbridge@iea.org.uk